PUBLIC ALTERNATIVE EDUCATION

Options and Choice for Today's Schools

TIMOTHY W. YOUNG

Teachers College, Columbia University
New York and London

To my mother

Marjorie Rose Daily Young

Published by Teachers College Press, 1234 Amsterdam Avenue
New York, NY 10027

Library of Congress Cataloging-in-Publication Data

Young, Timothy Wallace.
   Public alternative education : options and choice for today's
schools / Timothy W. Young.
     p.   cm.
   Includes bibliographical references (p.).
   ISBN: 0-8077-3024-6. ISBN: 0-8077-3023-8 (pbk.)
   1. Free schools—United States.   2. Non-formal education—United
States.   I. Title.
LB1029.F7Y58 1990
371'.04—dc20   90–30368
                                         CIP

Printed on acid-free paper

Manufactured in the United States of America

96 95 94 93 92 91 90   8 7 6 5 4 3 2 1

Contents

Foreword

The alternative school movement in public education is a reform effort that is not supposed to exist. It seemed to come out of nowhere, and for two decades it has been denounced and discounted and often dismissed as a passing educational fad. In the late 1960s, when alternative public schools first began to appear, they startled the educational establishment. They were neither the byproduct of some new federal program nor the brainchild of a university or foundation. No book had been written on the topic. And, with the exception of a few early articles by Mario Fantini calling for choice in public education, alternatives had not been described, researched, or conceptualized. It was long after the first schools were developed that the term *alternative public schools* came to be used. Emerging almost simultaneously throughout the country, the schools represented a truly unexpected grassroots movement.

During the early years, most believed that the existence of such schools was little more than an educational anomaly: a mirror image of the free school movement that had existed earlier outside of public education. Others dismissed the schools as the latest educational fad—a foolish fad, some maintained—that would flourish for a while, spawn a flurry of "cult-like" articles in scholarly journals, then fade away. But for slightly over two decades alternative public schools have continued to surprise American educators. Today, that "fad" not only survives, but seems to be growing in strength.

Alternative schools have also forced educational researchers to rethink many of the accepted tenets of the profession. Though on the surface a simple and obvious concept—providing choice and diversity within the monopolistic bureaucratic giant of public education—research on alternative schools continues to bring revelations.

Before alternative schools came along, we had naively concluded that the primary factor in educational change was the school principal. Based on "solid" Ford Foundation research, the profession had come to believe that if the principal of a "reformed" school moved on to another job, the school tended to slip back into more traditional ways. Alternative schools changed all of that. When the first generation of alternative school principals and directors moved on to new challenges, most observers were surprised that the schools continued to flourish. This unexpected result led to a decade of "effective school" research that provided a more realistic insight into the concept of lasting educational reform.

Before alternative schools, we believed that everyone learned in the same way and should be taught in the same way using a common curriculum. We thought all schools should be alike. We thought that children and their parents were incapable of making decisions about what and how they learned. We now know that we were wrong, that there is no single best way for all to learn. We also know that though open education worked for some, it is not necessarily best for all: Not everyone should be in the same traditional classroom, but the inverse is also true. Alternative schools helped us understand that different students could best learn in very different ways.

When alternative schools first appeared, they were developed in most instances by educational "true believer" types without the benefit of educational research to guide their efforts. Now, after twenty years of independent educational research there is a significant knowledge base to support the maintenance and expansion of alternative schools and to guide their future development. Researchers of public schools often discovered that their most positive data came from a small portion of their research population. Upon identifying the schools where this data was obtained they discovered, often for the first time, alternative schools.

Large numbers of independent studies led to basically the same conclusion: Alternative schools have unusually positive effects on students and their teachers. Students in alternative schools tend to learn better, feel better about themselves and about school, feel their needs are being met better than in traditional schools, have fewer absences, are less violent and disruptive and have more democratic attitudes. Especially for the dropout, the illiterate, the underachieving or disruptive student, alternative schools proved to be unusually effective. Such schools offered substantive proof for the first time that, given the right environment, all kids could indeed learn. Alternative schools have also been found to be the most effective, some would say only effective, strategy for achieving school desegregation.

We now know that alternative public schools work. They enable small groups of students, teachers, and parents to develop and utilize different educational strategies. This is an approach that has thus far had lasting effects. And, perhaps most remarkable, alternative schools represent an entire spectrum of educational possibilities: More than ten years ago, Vern Smith of Indiana University identified over 150 different types of alternative schools. Thus, we have today a wide variety of established educational models that have been evaluated as effective with certain students.

After ten years of research, hundreds of school evaluations, and countless observations in alternative schools throughout the United States and Canada, I am absolutely convinced that the most distinctive, exciting, and effective schools in America, both today and at any time in our nation's past are the alternative public schools that have been developed since the mid–1960s. Visit the St. Paul Open School, Philadelphia Parkway, or Vocational Village and the Metropolitan Learning Center, or performing arts schools in any of a dozen of the major cities in America, and you will find some of the most creative and refreshing schools that have ever existed. And, unlike so many other public schools, these programs have been carefully evaluated again and again. There have also been some follow-up evaluations of the graduates of these programs for four to eight years.

In the early 1970s, I had the good fortune of being at Indiana University and working with Vern Smith and Dan Burke. Depressed by a wave of macabre educational literature that included *Death at an Early Age, Our Children Are Dying, Crisis in the Classroom*—a Carnegie Report that was serialized in *Atlantic* magazine under the title "Murder in the Classroom"—we set out to find somewhere in America where school reform had worked, where schools were humane and effective, where students and their teachers worked together in a healthy harmony of learning. With a small grant from Dave Clark, then Dean of the Indiana University School of Education, we set out in search of good schools in America. Our search ultimately led to a small conference in Bloomington, Indiana, attended by approximately a dozen schools that seemed to us to reflect the best that we knew about learning in public education.

Excited by what we learned about these schools, which included the new Philadelphia Parkway School and a number of new schools in Berkeley, California, we expanded our search. Later, with funds from the Johnson Foundation, we invited over a hundred schools to a Wingspread Conference in Racine, Wisconsin. What was so interesting about the schools that we were identifying was that a large number of them had common, and for public schools very unusual, characteristics: Students and teachers chose to be in the schools, and the schools were dramatically different not only from the vast majority of

American schools but even from each other. What made them so distinctive was that these schools had been designed, planned, and implemented to address the needs of a specific group of students and/or developed on the basis of a particular philosophical concept of education.

During the next few years, Indiana University developed a national organization called Options in Public Education, a newsletter called *Changing Schools,* and a new graduate program that prepared teachers for their new and emerging roles in alternative public schools. We held over a hundred regional conferences and two international conferences on alternative education. We published the first national directory of alternative schools, conducted the first descriptive research, and began to write about our discoveries. Within a two year period, every major educational journal in America published a special issue on alternative public schools. Articles on alternative education soon began appearing in everything from *Good Housekeeping* to the *New York Times.* For a while we experienced the exhilaration of discovery and the excitement of reporting new phenomena. And we became more than objective education researchers; we championed the concept of alternative education. We consulted with school districts throughout the United States and our students became educational pioneers who helped start new alternative schools in Michigan, California, New York, Toronto, and Indiana. We testified before Congress and served as expert witnesses in desegregation cases in Denver and Louisville.

After investing a major portion of my professional life in the study of alternative schools, it gives me great personal satisfaction to witness the latest surge of interest in alternative public schools and a new book summarizing the movement. Just as the rebirth of interest in alternative schools was stimulated by desegregation efforts in the mid–1970s, a Senate Subcommittee on Violence and Vandalism of the late 1970s, Reagan's interest in voucher education in the early 1980s, the recent concern for at-risk youth has led once again to a renaissance of reform in public education alternatives. There is also a growing nationwide interest in developing options for all. The governor of Minnesota has developed a plan that permits every family to chose any school in the state. It is not surprising that one of the governor's key advisors is Joe Nathan, one of the original teachers of the St. Paul Open School.

This book by Tim Young represents the most recent and perhaps the best effort to summarize the alternative school movement and to provide the novice reader with a careful selection of some of the most interesting and unusual alternatives in America. The reader, however, should be warned. If you are a concerned educator and if you are learning about alternatives for the first time, you risk being caught up in an unexpected challenge regarding the potential for public education. This book may open the door to unanticipated possibilities. If you take this book and the schools it describes seriously, you will surely no longer be willing to accept your local schools as the status quo. You risk learning about a new world of educational possibilities that could indeed challenge your commitment and change your life. It could also lead to a dramatic change in the way children and youth in your own community are educated. If you are ready for such a challenge, then read on.

Robert D. Barr
School of Education
Oregon State University

Acknowledgments

I want to thank the teachers and administrators in the public alternative schools I visited for taking the time and interest to explain their programs to me. I particularly want to thank Jerry Altena (Environmental Education Program), John Anderson (Extended Learning Family), Phil Barber (Off-Campus), Wes Crago (Stanton), Paul Erickson (Vocational Village), Jay Hill (Learning Unlimited), Dorothy LeGault (Open School), and Keith Rose (Parkway).

The teachers and administrators in the Washington Alternative Learning Association (WALA) have taught me a great deal. Contributing to my education have been Chuck Abernathy, Jeff Evans, Bob Fizzell, Karol Gadwa, Bill Jennings, Harry Johnson, Nancy Messmer, Roy Morris, and Bill Wiley.

The time and support to complete the book were made possible by the Faculty Research Committee at Central Washington University, which awarded me a sabbatical and research grant. I am grateful to the committee for its support.

Two reviewers, Thomas Gregory of Indiana University and Peter McLaren of Miami University, made helpful suggestions to improve the final draft. Any shortcomings of the book, however, are my responsibility. I also want to thank Mary Anne Raywid of Hofstra University, who was kind enough to share materials and information with me.

Behind every successful writer is a good editor. I was fortunate to have two at Teachers College Press. Ron Galbraith gave me hope and confidence by showing an interest in my project and encouraging me along the way. Brian Ellerbeck's editing improved my writing.

Lastly, behind every successful man is a woman. In my case it is my wife, Harriet. She is my first editor and keeps me focused on the task at hand. My son Nicholas and daughter Alethea are my inspiration. It is my hope they will have a better public education than I did.

Introduction

As a public secondary social studies and English teacher from 1970 to 1976, I observed that the schools in which I taught were not meeting the needs of a large number of students. In fact, it was apparent to me that some students were not getting much from school at all. Most of these students were poor or disadvantaged, but many were not. Sensitive students, shy students, gifted students were among those who "fell between the cracks" and became lost. I must confess that I did little to reach such students. With my six daily classes of twenty-eight students each, I, like most teachers, channeled my time and energy toward reaching the needs of the majority, and for the most part, I was successful. However, I felt an uneasiness and sense of guilt about the students I had failed to serve. It became obvious to me that neither I nor the school could serve all students unless the structure of schooling underwent change. What those changes might be I had little idea.

While a graduate student at Indiana University, I took a course offered by Dr. Robert Barr (now Dean of the School of Education at Oregon State University), which gave me my first introduction to alternative education. It provided an overview and rationale for options in public schools. Additional coursework from Drs. Vernon Smith and Thomas Gregory expanded my introduction beyond alternative schools and programs to include alternative teaching and classroom strategies. A visit to Learning Unlimited (a school within a school option) in Indianapolis and a small dropout prevention program in Bloomington made concrete and gave meaning to the ideas I had been exposed to in my coursework.

These two very different alternative programs were similar in their attention to student interests and needs. Teachers and students were on a first-name basis and engaged in a cooperative rather than adversarial venture. Students were given individual attention and the flexibility to pursue coursework they had helped to design.

I received my doctorate from Indiana University in 1980 and moved to Washington state and Central Washington University in Ellensburg. The next year I became involved with the Washington Alternative Learning Association (WALA), an association of elementary and secondary teachers and administrators from public and private alternative schools and programs in Washington state. WALA is the largest and most active association of its kind in the country. It sponsors a state conference annually, publishes a highly regarded quarterly newsletter, *Options in Education,* and sponsored the 1987 National Conference on Alternative Education. Since 1981 I have been active in WALA, serving for a term on its executive board and visiting alternative schools and programs throughout the state. I have conducted several workshops in conjunction with teachers and administrators from WALA.

In 1987, I applied for and was granted a sabbatical by Central Washington University to further my study of alternative education. During the fall of 1987, I substitute taught in several public high schools in Los Angeles County. Most of my time was spent in a dropout prevention high school program. In the spring and fall of 1988, I visited a number of nationally known public alternative schools and programs, descriptions of which comprise Chapter 4 of this book. I also traveled extensively in Washington state, visiting numerous alternative schools and programs.

Public Alternative Education: Options and Choice for Today's Schools provides an introduction to public alternative education for parents, teachers, and administrators who might not be familiar with the concept or who have a passing but incomplete understanding of it. The book is meant to be a survey rather than a comprehensive examination of public alternative education; it is designed for use as a supplementary text in undergraduate and graduate foundations courses, and inservice courses for teachers and administrators.

Chapter 1 outlines the historical background of alternatives in public education. Chapter 2 offers the rationale for variety and choice in our public schools. Chapter 3 analyzes the effectiveness of public schools of choice and attempts to answer the question: Are these schools any good? Chapter 4 describes in detail six exemplary public alternative schools and programs. Chapter 5 details one community's attempt to serve at-risk students. Chapter 6 concludes with a look at the future direction of public alternative education as we move into the 1990s.

My visits to public alternative schools have convinced me of the importance and effectiveness of options and choice within public education. I have seen dedicated teachers and administrators assist students for whom no one, including their parents, cared. I have seen alternative programs provide gifted students with the freedom to take risks and to challenge themselves beyond what a conventional school could offer. I have seen Hispanic young men attend an evening alternative program to learn English and obtain their GED after having worked all day in the fields. I have seen unwed teenage mothers gain the necessary academic skills and self-esteem to become economically and psychologically self-sufficient.

Public alternative schools serve these and other students well. They do it more effectively and more cheaply than conventional public schools. Since their introduction in the late 1960s and early 1970s, options within public education have grown dramatically. They can no longer be written off as a fad or frill. They represent an idea whose time has come. Public alternative schools and programs merit our attention and support. That is why I have written this book.

ONE

The Development of Alternatives in Public Education

Some observers have described the 1980s as "the education decade." Not since the 1950s have the general public and the popular media focused such attention on the nation's schools. While much of the attention has been critical, the effect has been to encourage a rethinking of the role and structure of schooling. Conservatives have been particularly vocal in their criticism of the public schools, but liberals, too, have expressed dissatisfaction with America's public education system. Pressures from both right and left are forcing schools to experiment more with nontraditional approaches to teaching and learning in an attempt to improve their effectiveness.

Parents are asking for greater variety and increased participation and freedom of choice in the educational programs their children may pursue. Alternatives, or options within public education, are gaining in credibility and popularity as school districts move to incorporate the concepts of variety and choice within their systems.

The concept of public schools of choice has drawn increased national attention and support. In January 1989, then President-elect Bush declared at the White House Workshop on Choice in Education his support for choice in public education:

> Certainly among the most promising of these ideas—perhaps the single most promising of these ideas—is choice. It responds to a simple but quite serious problem. In most places around the country . . . students are arbitrarily assigned by their school systems to a single school. If that school is a bad one, its students are trapped.
>
> Choice plans that are intelligently conceived, implemented, and monitored—plans like magnet schools, open enrollment programs, and other innovative mechanisms—restore that opportunity to our families. ("Perhaps the single most promising reform idea," 1989, p. 24)

1

Upon assuming office President Bush acted on his previous declaration with a $100 million program to expand public magnet schools and parental choice as part of his first budget proposal to Congress. The call for increased parental choice and options within public education was one of the recommendations made by the President and a number of the nation's governors at the historic education summit at the University of Virginia in October, 1989.

Options and choice in public education have become "hot" topics not only among educational practitioners and theorists but also among politicians and the general public. Some see public schools of choice as the solution to America's declining educational fortunes. Others fear that alternatives in public education represent just another short-lived fad. Before deciding which view, if either, is correct, it is important to have an understanding of public alternative education.

WHAT ARE PUBLIC ALTERNATIVE SCHOOLS?

According to one expert, the term *public alternative school* means "any school that provides alternative learning experiences to those provided by conventional schools and that is available by choice to every family within its community at no extra cost" (Smith, 1974, pp. 14–15). Alternative schools are distinguished from their conventional counterparts by the following characteristics:

- A greater responsiveness to a perceived educational need within the community.
- A more focused instructional program, usually featuring a particular curricular emphasis, instructional method, or school climate.
- A shared sense of purpose. Common goals and a defined educational philosophy are held by students and staff.
- A more student-centered philosophy. Emphasis is on the whole student. Affective as well as cognitive needs are met.
- A noncompetitive environment. Students are not pitted against one another for grades and recognition. Student progress is measured in terms of self-improvement.
- A greater autonomy. Principals, teachers, and students have greater freedom from the central administration than their counterparts in traditional schools.

- A smaller school and a more personalized relationship between students and staff.

According to the U.S. Department of Justice, an alternative education program,

> embraces subject matter and/or teaching methodology that is not generally offered to students of the same age or grade level in traditional school settings, which offers a range of educational options and includes the student as an integral part of the planning team. The term includes the use of program methods and materials that facilitate students success and are relevant to students' needs and interests. (U.S. Department of Justice, 1980, p. 11)

Unlike conventional public schools, alternative schools do not attempt to be all things to all people. In consumer terms, they are specialty shops rather than department stores. They usually offer programs that are designed for and serve a target population (e.g., dropouts, teenage parents, students with a vocational/career orientation, the gifted/talented, etc). Because of this focus they can be more effective in meeting the needs of a particular population.

The options within alternative education are quite varied today. They include schools without walls; schools within schools; learning centers; multicultural, fundamental, continuation, residential, and open schools. In addition, magnet schools offer a number of theme and specialty programs for purposes of integration. The concept of alternative education is not a new idea. A variety of educational options and choice can be found as far back as the colonial period in American history.

EARLY ALTERNATIVES IN AMERICAN EDUCATION

Alternatives in American education are as old as the country itself. The most popular educational option in colonial America was instruction at home. Most children learned informally from parents and relatives, but colonists also established a variety of public and private schools to provide a formal education to serve the needs of their children. Within the public schools several options existed, representing different levels of content and quality. At the top were grammar schools for middle- and upper-class boys. These schools operated year round and featured a classical curriculum that included instruction in Latin and Greek. In the middle were common schools for middle- and lower-class boys and girls. These schools operated for a few months during the year, offering an English-based curriculum and emphasizing the three R's. At the bottom were charity schools for poor and minority children. These schools provided an abbreviated program in basic literacy. Perhaps the best-known graduate of a charity school was Benjamin Banneker, who attended a school operated by the Philadelphia Society for the Propagation of the Gospel.

During the seventeenth and eighteenth centuries private schools greatly outnumbered public ones. A variety of options existed for students who could afford to pay fees ranging from expensive to modest. Most expensive were private grammar schools, which catered to advantaged boys who wanted a classical curriculum and the opportunity to pursue higher education. At the modest level were dame schools. Women operated these schools out of their home, offering young boys and girls training in domestic skills and instruction in the three R's. Older boys who wanted to learn a trade or specialized skill chose among the many entrepreneurial schools, which provided vocational training at various levels of cost and quality. At the bottom were private charity schools, which served the same disadvantaged clientele as their public counterparts. They charged no fee and were supported by church and missionary groups.

An additional option was introduced in 1751 by Benjamin Franklin, who wanted to provide an alternative to the classical curriculum of the grammar school. He established an academy in Philadelphia for talented older boys who did not intend to pursue higher education but wanted a general preparation for careers in commerce and business. The school's curriculum was English-based and included accounting, drawing, and mechanics as well as more general subjects. It is from the academy that our present-day comprehensive public high school has evolved.

During the nineteenth century, enrollment in public education surpassed home and private instruction as the common elementary school became the choice of parents and children. Educational leaders such as Henry Barnard of Connecticut, Caleb Mills of Indiana, and Samuel Lewis of Ohio worked successfully to sell the idea of a "free" common school education for children in their states. The most famous advocate of the common school, however, was Horace Mann, Secretary of the State Board of Education in Massachusetts.

Motivated by an almost religious intensity, Mann worked tirelessly to increase funding for and lengthening of the school year from twelve to sixteen weeks. He introduced such innovations as teacher training and pupil testing. Convinced of the rightness of his mission, Mann enthusiastically declared in 1840: "This institution is the greatest discovery ever made by man: we repeat it, the common school is the greatest discovery ever made by man" (quoted in Perkinson, 1976, p. 110).

Not all Americans shared Mann's unqualified support for the common school. An outspoken critic and contemporary of Mann's was Ralph Waldo Emerson. His assessment of public education and the common school, written in 1840, shared none of Mann's enthusiasm:

> Our education, like other institutions and formularies of the present age is poor. It has no breadth. It speaks in a dialect. As we construe it, education refers to a narrow circle of experiences, powers, and literature of its own. Education should be as broad as man and demonstrating whatever elements are in him. . . . Today's education does none of this. We confront the vanity of our education when we look at its result: society. (quoted in Perkinson, 1976, p. 110)

While Mann emphasized the social functions of public education, Emerson focused on the needs of the individual. Mann wanted common schools to teach values and skills that would contribute to an orderly and productive society. Emerson was more interested in individual freedom than in social order and worried that common schools contributed to needless conformity at the expense of personal growth. Interestingly, these two points of view still constitute a major debate in public education today.

Attempts to reform education were undertaken by a number of individuals and groups in the nineteenth century. Two of the better known reform attempts were by Bronson Alcott and Robert Owen. Alcott, a friend of Emerson and fellow transcendentalist, established the Temple School in Boston. The school's curriculum was traditional in format but not in content. Students were encouraged to pursue self-knowledge. They were never criticized for thinking, even if their thoughts were in conflict with Alcott's. Self-reflection and analysis were undertaken in journal writing and Socratic dialogue. Owen, the noted British textile mill owner and philanthropist, founded a utopian community in New Harmony, Indiana. Here one of the first kindergartens in America was established as well as a school for older students that was self-supporting and featured a vocational and agricultural skills curriculum. New Harmony and Temple School were short-lived experiments, however, and had little impact on educational practices of the day.

Parochial Schools

A more enduring alternative to the public common school was the establishment and growth of the Catholic parochial school system in the middle and latter parts of the nineteenth century. Catholic parents, many of them newly arrived immigrants, were dissatisfied with what they saw as the control of public education by Protestants. Catholic clergy, such as Archbishop John Hughes of New York, publicly attacked religious bias in the schools and argued for a more pluralistic educational philosophy, but they were unsuccessful. As a result the Catholic Church created a parochial system of education to parallel the public one.

In 1884 the Third Plenary Council of American Catholic Bishops declared that all parishes were to build parochial schools and that all parents were to send their children to them unless exempted by the Church. By 1890 42 percent of Catholic parishes had schools, which enrolled more than 633,000 students (McCluskey, 1969). Protestant sects dissatisfied with public education also established parochial schools, but their numbers were very small. Parochial education continues as a viable private alternative to public education today. In 1987, about 2.7 million students were enrolled in 9,120 Catholic schools, constituting about 7 percent of all K–12 students (Pavuk, 1987).

The Progressive Education Movement

Innovations and options within public education were introduced during the late nineteenth and gained support in the early twentieth century with the popularity of the progressive education movement. Progressive educators shared with their mentor, John Dewey, a belief in child-centered education, experiential learning activities, and democratic classroom practices. Programs in Quincy and Dalton, Massachusetts, Gary, Indiana, and Winnetka, Illinois, were among the more prominent examples of progressive innovation.

In the 1870s Quincy abandoned the set curriculum and developed teacher-made materials to replace texts. In 1907 Gary established extended-year schools that functioned as miniature communities. Elementary and secondary students were housed in the same building and worked on both in- and out-of-school projects as part of their course of study. In the 1920s Dalton and Winnetka introduced a combination of individualized study and group work. In Dalton rooms became laboratories where students worked on individual contracts in their academic subjects part of the day and experienced whole-group instruction in nonacademic subjects during the remainder. In Winnetka grade promotion and failing as such were eliminated. Students worked in self-paced learning packets in the morning and undertook group and creative activities in the afternoon.

These and other experiments attempted to expand the traditional curriculum by integrating real-life experiences with academic material. The use of unit plans and the project method encouraged an interdisciplinary approach to learning. Rather than studying subjects in isolation from one another, a student could, under a theme or project such as "transportation," study math related to the mileage and measurement of travel. English could include vocabulary, spelling, and reading comprehension from literature on transportation. Science might focus on mechanics of movement and design, and art could include drawings of boats, planes, and trains.

Community-based learning was also encouraged by progressive reformers. Field trips to sites related to the theme or project being studied were undertaken. In addition, students might receive credit for participating in such community projects as beautifying a neighborhood park, assisting in the local YMCA, or volunteering at a nursery school. These activities were designed to bring the school and community closer together and promote democratic ideals.

Within progressive classrooms a degree of choice was encouraged. Learning centers in the elementary classroom allowed children to work in small groups or alone on various topics of interest designed by the teacher. At the secondary level, course electives such as typing, commercial law, social studies, fine and practical arts, and domestic science, as well as such extracurricular activities as student clubs and interscholastic athletics, were introduced to offer choices and generate student interest.

The progressive education movement was in part a response to the industrialization of America and the increased participation of children in public education. In 1890, while most 6- to 12-year-olds were attending elementary schools, only 7 percent of 14- to 17-year-olds were enrolled in high school. By 1930, enrollment of 14- to 17-year-olds was 51 percent. The enormous increase in secondary school enrollment and the diversity of the student body put added pressure on schools to expand and democratize the curriculum.

At the high school more vocational options were introduced. The federal government took an active role in encouraging this development. The Smith-Hughes Act (1917) provided money for home economics, agriculture, trade, and industrial subjects. The George-Dean Act (1937) added distributive education.

While industrialism gave impetus to the progressive education movement, its larger effect was the standardization of public education through the adoption of "scientific" curricular and instructional practices. Today's conventional educational practices, such as group testing, ability-group tracking, age-specific grade levels, and teaching by objectives, were all innovations brought about by industrialism.

EDUCATIONAL REFORM IN THE 1960s AND 1970s

The progressive education movement faltered in the 1940s due in part to excesses in experimentation, Americans' short attention span for educational reform, and World War II. It died in the 1950s because of the Cold War and the successful launching of Sputnik by the Soviets in 1957. The demonstration of Soviet expertise in space took the emphasis away from individual student interests and child-centered instruction, placing it instead on national interests and subject-centered instruction. Public education became primarily a means for competing with the Soviets for technological superiority. Curricula became more prescribed and academic in focus. The National Defense Education Act (1958) provided money for materials and instruction in math, science, and foreign languages, subjects deemed to be in the national interest. Curricular reforms of the late 1950s and early 1960s, such as School Math Study Group (SMSG), Biological Science Curriculum Study (BSCS), and Chemical Education Material Society (CHEM), were designed primarily for the talented 15–20 percent of students. Schools became more competitive as students were increasingly grouped by ability into college preparatory, business, vocational, and general tracks. Students could choose among these options, but much of the choice was made for them by guidance counselors using students' test results.

The new emphasis on competition and serving the nation's manpower needs was not without its detractors, however. Paul Goodman in *Compulsory Mis-education and the Community of Scholars* (1964a) and *Growing up Absurd* (1964b), and Edgar Friedenberg in *The Vanishing Adolescent* (1959), argued that children were being schooled rather than educated. According to them, public schools socialized the young to accept national norms and to fit into the country's manpower needs rather than providing a moral and intellectual education that fostered personal growth. Schools served to confirm social-class distinctions and promote a narrow economic function for acquiring an education. Students, especially the poor and less successful, became alienated from school and society and developed a negative sense of self.

A second criticism arose from those concerned with the increasing emphasis on academic excellence. They felt schools were defining excellence solely in narrow cognitive terms at the expense of equity. The concern for equity or fairness could be traced back to the civil rights movement, which had gained national prominence in the 1950s. The 1954 Supreme Court decision in *Brown* v *Board of Education* required schools to welcome and serve children from all racial and ethnic backgrounds. As a result, the issue of equity or equality was added to the demand for excellence in the national debate on public education.

Complementing the issue of racial and ethnic equality was the concern for economic equality. In the 1960s America undertook a war on poverty and made schools the battlefield. In 1965 Congress passed the Elementary and Secondary Education Act as President Johnson declared, "The answer for all our national problems—the answer for all the problems of the world—comes down to one word, that word is education" (quoted in *Education Almanac*, 1984, p. 114).

Equity gradually replaced excellence as national educational policies focused increasingly on socially and economically disadvantaged students. Writers such as Frank Riessman, in *The Culturally Deprived Child* (1962), emphasized the academic potential of disadvantaged children and urged schools to be sensitive to cultural pluralism. The relevance of an academic and cognitively oriented curriculum based on middle-class values for minority and poor children was called into question by Gerald Weinstein and Mario Fantini in *Toward Humanistic Education* (1970). They challenged schools to become more meaningful to the disadvantaged by developing a curriculum of affect. Schools and teachers were being increasingly encouraged to experiment with alternative programs and teaching strategies to reach a more diverse student population.

Support for the earlier criticisms of Goodman and Friedenberg grew dramatically in the mid to late 1960s, in large part because of the Vietnam War. The war provoked widespread dissatisfaction with national manpower needs and disillusionment over the apparent gap between the national government's professed and actual goals. The result was a critical reassessment of America's political, social, and economic institutions during this decade. Public education underwent one of the most critical institutional reassessments. Schools were seen by many as a primary cause for the country's social, political, and economic ills. A group of writers dubbed the "romantic critics" pointed out the defects in public education and called for dramatic changes in the education of children.

Jonathan Kozol (*Death at an Early Age*, 1967), Nat Hentoff (*Our Children are Dying*, 1967), and Herbert Kohl (*36 Children*, 1967) portrayed public schools as racist. John Holt (*How Children Learn*, 1967; *How Children Fail*, 1964) criticized the predetermined curriculum of school and students' dependence on the teacher as the complete intellectual authority. Holt attacked the emphasis on producing right answers at the expense of reflection and curiosity. Neil Postman and Charles Weingartner (*Teaching as a Subversive Activity*, 1971b; *The School Book*, 1973) maintained that traditional teaching was authoritarian. Teachers told students what they thought students ought to know and think and rarely encouraged student-initiated questions or responses. Postman and Weingartner pointed out that the information schools transmitted was in large part obsolete because of the knowledge explosion. They argued that students needed to learn how, not what. Ivan Illich (*Deschooling Society*, 1971) decried the institutional dependency that public education fostered and proposed to abolish schools altogether.

Romantic critics split into a variety of camps. Some worked for change within the system and became reformers. Others, such as writer Allen Graubard (*Free the Children*), became radicals rejecting public schools and proposing independent free schools in their place. In Graubard's words, change was impossible within the system because "The problems are basically rooted in the social conditions and not in the schools. The problems are manifested in the schools, but they aren't created there and they can't be solved there. . . . Schools must run up against the fundamental social realities—the sickness of American society" (1972, pp. 259–260).

Free schools sought a new direction in education. They rejected authority and embraced freedom. Their educational philosophy rested on a romantic view of the child best expressed by A. S. Neill, the founder of Summerhill: "My view is that a child is innately wise and realistic, if left to himself without adult suggestion of any kind, he will develop as far as he is capable of developing" (1960, p. 4).

Free schools offered students a great deal of choice. The curriculum was likely to include folk dancing, history of drugs, guerrilla theater, jewelry making, black and women's liberation as well as more traditional subjects. Teachers were guides rather than authorities.

They assisted students with learning but did not impose it on them. In the words of one free school teacher: "I don't want to lay my trip on any of these kids. If they really want to learn something, they'll come to me and say, 'Look man, I want to get into this, can you help me?' If they say that to me, then that's cool. If not, I'm not going to force them. That's a public school trip" (Graubard, 1972, p. 11).

The free school movement never gained widespread acceptance. The number of free schools peaked at several hundred in the mid-1970s. Their existence was always precarious and their lifespan short. The difficulty of meeting expenses while maintaining continuity and commitment made instability inevitable. As the Vietnam War wound down in the 1970s, some of the ideological urgency was lost and radicalism became more difficult to sustain.

While radicals chose the hard revolution, reformers preferred the soft. They saw teaching as a subversive activity to be conducted within public education rather than a revolutionary one to be conducted outside it. They focused on options that could be adopted by public schools. The most popular option advanced by reformers in the late 1960s and early 1970s was open education.

Joseph Featherstone (1967a, 1967b, 1967c) introduced informal or open education to Americans in a series of articles written for *The New Republic*. Featherstone described and praised the education he had observed in England's infant, or primary, schools. In these schools children worked at their own pace and frequently on their own. Progress was evaluated in terms of individual improvement rather than by comparison to a standard or to the performance of others. Students were allowed some choice in the subjects they studied. Teachers assisted student learning rather than controlling it.

In actuality, open education was little more than a rediscovery of the philosophy of the progressive education movement. Both approaches assumed children were curious, responsible, and motivated to learn and should be allowed to develop at their own rates. Both advocated a child-centered approach that built on students' interests. Learning experiences were to be more concrete, and students were to be encouraged to move about and engage in hands-on activities.

Open education also drew heavily from the earlier nongraded or continuous school programs that had developed during the late 1940s and early 1950s. These schools practiced cross-age grouping of children with similar ability into three-year blocks with the same teacher. Children progressed at their own rates and could complete the primary block in two years instead of the usual three if they were clever or take four years if they were not. Individualized instruction was at the heart of the program, but teachers exercised control over the curricular content. The vast majority of nongraded schools were elementary, and most of those were primary. A few nongraded secondary schools had been attempted. Two of the better known ones were Nova and Melbourne High Schools in Florida. B. Frank Brown's *The Nongraded High School* (1963) details the inception and operation of Melbourne High School.

While most of the experimentation with open education occurred in elementary schools, effects began to be felt at the secondary level. Public high schools featuring an open education were started in Newton, Massachusetts, in 1967, Portland, Oregon, in 1969, and St. Paul, Minnesota, in 1971.

Murray Road Annex in Newton enrolled 100 students. Classes met during the morning three days a week to allow students time to pursue out-of-school experiences. Instead of grades and report cards, teacher evaluations and student self-evaluations were used. Students also participated in school governance.

John Adams High School in Portland enrolled 1,300 students. For half the day students worked in ungraded, non-ability-grouped teams on such topics of social interest as pollution, welfare and unemployment, student unrest, and crime. Academic subjects were taught in conjunction with the interdisciplinary topics. Student and faculty senates were responsible for school governance.

St. Paul Open School, with 500 students, featured an individualized, competency-based program of study in seven major resource areas (art, music/drama, industrial arts, physical education, home economics, math/science, and humanities). Instead of grades, students received credits for demonstrated competencies in various skill areas, such as information finding, career awareness, communications, and cultural and community awareness.

With the acceptance of open education, public schools began to experiment with a variety of options in the late 1960s and early 1970s. Among the most popular were schools without walls, schools within a school, multicultural schools, continuation schools, and learning centers.

TYPES OF PUBLIC ALTERNATIVES

Schools

Schools without walls. In 1969 the Parkway School in Philadelphia and Community High School in Berkeley became the first two schools without walls. Both featured a program of community-based learning experiences and incorporated community resource people as instructors.

Philadelphia Parkway (as it's commonly known), the more famous and more durable of the two, was financed initially by a Ford Foundation grant. The first year the school enrolled 140 students. By the second year it had expanded to three units of 160 students each. Within each unit or community, tutorials of sixteen students, a teacher, and a university intern were established. Tutorials met four hours weekly for counseling and basic skills instruction in language and math. The remainder of a student's time was spent in required coursework for graduation taught by Parkway staff and in electives and independent study using the city as the curriculum. Classes were located in various businesses, banks, museums, and community agencies and were taught in large part by community resource people. Students worked toward credits rather than toward grades. They also shared in school governance through weekly town meetings in each unit. Philadelphia Parkway caught the imagination of educational reformers and for many became *the* symbol of public alternative education. Other schools without walls followed: Metro High in Chicago, Shanti School in Hartford, City School in Madison and Walden II in Racine, Wisconsin. By 1972 schools without walls had become the most popular option, comprising 22 percent of public alternative schools.

Schools within a school.   Schools within a school was an innovative option developed primarily at the secondary level to break down the size and numbers of large comprehensive high schools into more manageable and humane units. In 1969 Pilot School was created in Cambridge, Massachusetts, within the regular comprehensive high school. Pilot School provided a more informal learning atmosphere with an emphasis on cross-cultural education for its 200 students, who had had difficulty adjusting to a large urban high school.

The most ambitious and best known of the schools within a school was established in Quincy, Illinois, in 1972. Quincy II High School enrolled 1,500 students in a complex of seven schools within a school. Each school featured a program designed to match students' learning styles and interests. Students could choose from programs in fine arts; special education; traditional, career, or individualized study; work-study; and flexible modular scheduling.

Schools within a school were also developed at the elementary level. In 1969 a group of parents in Arlington, Massachusetts, dissatisfied with the traditional elementary school their children attended, lobbied successfully for open classrooms, initially in grades K–2, to parallel traditional ones within the school. As their children moved into the intermediate grades, the open classroom option was expanded to include all grades. In 1973 parents in Cupertino, California, also lobbied successfully for an option within the district's elementary schools. This time the option desired was a conservative one. Parents were able to have "academics-plus" classrooms established within several of the regular elementary schools. These classrooms offered a more academically structured and disciplined approach to instruction, including a dress code, regularly scheduled homework, few fieldtrips, and a teacher-centered approach to instruction.

Multicultural schools. Multicultural schools were designed to serve students from a variety of ethnic and racial backgrounds with curricula that emphasized cultural pluralism. Classes in black and Chicano studies, Swahili and Spanish, international cooking and folk dance were integrated into the traditional curriculum. Coursework in human relations was another important component of these schools.

While some multicultural schools, such as Agora in Berkeley and Palmer School in Grand Rapids, had an ethnically diverse student body, most served a particular ethnic or racial group. Marcus Garvey Institute and Alliance Black House (both in Berkeley) served black students. Franklin, also in Berkeley, served Asian students. SAND Everywhere in Hartford enrolled primarily black and Puerto Rican students.

Continuation schools. Continuation schools provided an option for dropouts, potential dropouts, pregnant students, and teenage parents. They were designed to provide a less competitive, more individualized approach to learning. Programs varied but usually included individualized learning packages, contracts, nongraded or continuous progress, and behavior modification techniques. Continuation schools predated the open education movement. Metropolitan Youth Education Center in Denver and Pacific Shores High School in Manhattan Beach, California, were both started in 1964. Walbridge Academy in Grand Rapids opened in 1965. By 1972 continuation schools had become the second most popular option, representing 21 percent of public alternative schools.

Learning centers. Learning centers provided special resources and programs concentrated in one location. Centers existed for both elementary and secondary students. Most centers at the secondary level were vocational or technical in nature and included career awareness and preparation. Elementary centers typically offered high-interest enrichment programs to attract students for part of the day. Skyline in Dallas, John Dewey High School in Brooklyn, and St. Paul Learning Centers in St. Paul were among the better-known learning centers.

From 1970 to 1975 public alternative schools grew from a few hundred to more than 1,000. A survey of these schools conducted by Robert Barr (1975, p. 9) revealed the following breakdown of options within alternative schools:

Continuation schools	20%
Learning centers	18%
Schools within schools	17%
Open schools	15%
Schools without walls	6%
Multicultural schools	4%
Free schools	3%
Others	17%

Results of the 1975 survey indicated that the initial enthusiasm for schools without walls had waned considerably. This option had dropped from 22 percent to 6 percent of public alternative schools between 1972 and 1975. Continuation schools remained popular during this time period, declining by only 1 percent and becoming the most frequent option in 1975. Alternative schools were undergoing a gradual change as the country moved into more politically and economically conservative times.

Fundamental schools. Another option within public alternative schools was introduced in the mid-1970s and became extremely popular throughout the remainder of the decade. That option was the fundamental, or academics-plus, school. This type of school was created as a conservative alternative to the more progressive or liberal options that had typically characterized alternative schools. Parents and school officials who were uncomfortable with some of the experimentation in public education lobbied for an option that emphasized a back-to-basics curriculum and teacher-directed instruction. As mentioned earlier, Cupertino, California, created a fundamental school within a school option for parents in its district.

John Marshall Fundamental School in Pasadena was the best-known fundamental school and the first of its type at the secondary level. It began as a K–12 school in 1973 and split into elementary (K–5) and secondary (6–12) schools in 1975. The school required homework, gave letter grades, established a dress code, and enforced strict discipline. Ability grouping was practiced, and social promotions were not allowed.

Many school districts developed fundamental, or academics-plus, alternative schools in the late 1970s in response to a more conservative educational climate nationwide. By 1978 there were some 200 fundamental schools, making them the fastest-growing option in public alternative education.

Magnet schools.   School desegregation was the impetus for the development of yet another option in public education. In 1971 the Supreme Court, in *Swann v Charlotte-Mecklenberg*, legalized busing for the purpose of racially integrating public schools. The result was considerable tension in America's major cities and white flight to the suburbs. Forced busing met resistance primarily from white parents but also from minority parents whose children had to bear the burden of transportation.

When Minneapolis was ordered to desegregate its schools in 1972, the federal court exempted the district's four alternative schools because they had been successful in attracting a racially diverse student population. This became the first court sanctioning of magnet schools. In 1973 the Supreme Court allowed magnet schools to be used in the desegregation of Denver's public schools and in 1975 in the desegregation of Houston's public schools. The concept of magnet schools was fully institutionalized by 1975, when the federal court established an entire magnet district enrolling 25 percent of Boston's public school population.

Magnets were schools that received additional funding and resources to provide distinctive programs of study or special curricula in order to attract students from all racial groups within a school district and thus promote integration. Like the learning centers that preceded them, magnet schools concentrated resources in one location and usually featured a theme or area of emphasis.

Theme or specialty schools were not new to public education, particularly at the secondary level. Most major cities had specialty high schools for the academically, artistically, or technically talented. The oldest specialty high school was Boston Latin, founded in 1635. Other long-standing specialty schools were New York's Bronx High School of Science, Chicago's Lane Tech, San Francisco's Lowell High, and Philadelphia's Central High. These high schools were extremely selective, however, and based admittance on competitive examination results.

Magnet schools developed in the 1970s were, for the most part, nonselective. They were designed to promote integration and used race rather than ability as the criterion for student selection. A U.S. Department of Education study of a number of magnet schools conducted in 1983 found that only 33 percent of them used selective criteria such as grades, tests, and grade-point average for admittance (Blank, 1984).

Magnet schools grew rapidly in the late 1970s. By the 1981–82 school year some 1,200 were in operation. Approximately 60 percent of the options were at the elementary level, 10 percent at middle or junior high, and 30 percent at the high school level. An *Education Week* article (Snider, 1987) based on the Department of Education survey of 300 magnet schools in 1982 revealed the following distribution of themes or programs within the schools:[1]

Fundamental/academic	28%
Fine arts	14%
Vocational/career	11%
Individualized	11%
Science/math	10%
Multicultural/bilingual	9%
Humanities/social science	5%
Others	12%

Educational Vouchers

While radicals sought change outside public education and reformers sought reform from within, conservatives proposed an alternative that incorporated aspects of both. In 1962 Milton Friedman, the noted libertarian economist, introduced the idea of vouchers in his book *Capitalism and Freedom* (1962). Friedman proposed that parents be given a credit, or voucher, worth the amount the state spent to educate a child in the public schools. Parents would then be free to spend that amount on any public or private educational alternative of their choice. Friedman's proposal drew support from such liberals as Christopher Jencks (1970) and Henry Levin (1983), who saw vouchers as a way for disadvantaged parents to escape the hopelessness of ur-

---

[1]Reprinted with permission from *Education Week*, 6(39), June 24, 1987, p. C19.

ban public schools. Other supporters, like John Coons and Stephen Sugarman (1978), argued that vouchers would be beneficial for families of at-risk students: "In our opinion a significant proportion among the dropout and truant cadres would today be engaged in some organized pursuit of the minimum had they not been effectively expelled from that pursuit by compulsory assignment to a school experience they plainly despised" (p. 69).

In 1971 the Office of Economic Opportunity funded a four-year demonstration project of the voucher proposal in the Alum Rock, California, school district. Parents were allowed to use their vouchers only in the district's public schools. A little more than half of the district's schools participated. Because of limitations of the project, few conclusive results could be determined. A Rand Corporation study (*A Study of Alternatives . . .* , 1981) indicated teacher morale had increased, as had student and parent participation in the alternative schools. Academic achievement, however, was unaffected. Alum Rock was the first and last experiment with educational vouchers.

In 1983 the Reagan administration resurrected vouchers by proposing that a $600 credit be given to parents of poor children to be used to purchase a private education if they so desired. Congress rejected the proposal. In 1988, Secretary of Education William Bennett suggested Catholic schools be reimbursed by the states for each hardcore, at-risk student they enrolled. Despite the efforts of the Reagan administration, vouchers did not gain the political support necessary to become a viable option for parents and students.

Public opinion is divided fairly evenly on the issue. In 1987 44 percent of Americans supported the voucher system while 41 percent did not. In 1983, those figures had been 51 percent for and 41 percent against (Gallup & Clark, 1987). It would appear that support for educational vouchers, particularly those which include private school options, is currently waning. However, some interesting variations of the voucher idea can be found in a few states today and will be discussed further in Chapters 2 and 4.

ALTERNATIVE EDUCATION IN THE 1980s

As the 1980s began, alternative schools were firmly established in America's public education system. According to Mary Anne Raywid (1981), an estimated 10,000 public alternative schools were providing a variety of options to some 3 million students in 1981. Many of the alternative schools and programs that had been established in

the 1960s and early 1970s were no longer functioning Among the cu-
sualties were some of the best known: Chicago Metro, John Adams,
Murray Road Annex, Community High, Quincy II, and Melbourne
High School. (For a description of the demise of two of those schools,
see Richard Doremus' 1981, 1982 *Phi Delta Kappan* articles.) They were
replaced by many more, however. The new options were often less
experimental, reflecting a more conservative educational climate and
a different student clientele.

In the most recent survey to date (Raywid, 1982, p. 29) of public
alternative schools, conducted in 1981, respondents from 1,200 public
alternative secondary schools indicated the following distribution of
options:

Separate schools	38%
Schools within a school	20%
Remedial/corrective schools	13%
Satellite/annex schools	9%
Course offerings within parent school	8%
Schools maintained by several districts	3%
Schools without walls	1%
Others	8%

The 1981 survey was of secondary schools only, and many of the
categories are different from Barr's 1975 survey, so comparison is difficult. Three categories, "separate school," "school maintained by several districts," and "satellite/annex school," do not indicate the type of
option offered. These three categories make up 50 percent of the
sample. Schools without walls continued to lose support, declining
from 6 percent in 1975 to 1 percent in 1981, while schools within a
school became more popular, growing from 17 percent to 20 percent
during that time. The "remedial/corrective school," which characterized 13 percent of the options, is related to the "continuation school"
category in the 1975 survey.

While no national survey of public alternative schools has been
conducted since 1981, a recent survey (Young, 1988, p. 11) of 104 of
Washington state's public elementary and secondary alternative programs conducted by the author revealed the following distribution
within that state:

Continuation school	35%
School within a school or mini school	15%
Fundamental or academics-plus school	12%

Separate school	6%
Learning or resource center	6%
School without walls	2%
Multicultural or bilingual school	2%
Evening school	2%
Open school	1%
Free school	1%
Others	18%

Some caution is in order when drawing comparisons between the national and Washington surveys. First, the Washington sample includes both elementary and secondary schools, while the national sample is limited to secondary schools. Second, Washington may or may not be representative of the country. With those cautions noted, results from the two surveys indicate that options have changed from the more progressive and open orientation in the 1970s to a more conservative and remedial one in the 1980s. The continuation school, which is designed primarily for dropout prevention and to educate pregnant teenagers, is by far the most popular option, representing more than one-third of the alternative schools in Washington. On the other hand, schools without walls, free schools, and open schools represent less than 5 percent of the options within the state. Additionally, the fundamental, or academics-plus, school is the third most popular option, constituting 12 percent of the alternative schools. These changes are, in part, a reflection of the more conservative climate in the 1980s, but they are also a reflection of the fact that 69 percent of the schools in the 1981 national survey and 61 percent of the schools in the 1988 Washington survey indicated their students were functioning below local achievement levels.

The perception of the kinds of students served by public alternative schools and programs has also changed considerably during this past decade. When asked "What kind of student does your district's central administration associate with alternative education?", 73 percent of the respondents in the national survey said "all kinds," another 20 percent said "low achievers," "disruptive," or "turned off or disinterested" (Raywid, 1982, p. 29). When the same question was asked in the Washington survey, only 38 percent of respondents chose "all kinds," while 53 percent selected "low achievers," "disruptive," or "turned off" to describe the perception of alternative education among central administrators (Young, 1988, p. 11). These figures represent a rather substantial change in the clientele and rationale for public alternative education from its beginnings in the 1960s.

Growth of public alternative schools and programs in the 1980s is difficult to determine. Accurate statistics on the number of public alternative schools and student enrollment currently are not available. One can only estimate the number. One of the few states to keep a relatively accurate count of alternative schools during this decade is Washington. The Office of Superintendent of Public Instruction in cooperation with the Washington Alternative Learning Association publishes a directory of the state's alternative schools biannually. In 1981 the directory listed 52 public alternative education schools with combined enrollment of 6,274 students. In 1988 the number of schools had risen to 104 and enrollment to 9,945, a growth rate of over 60 percent. During that same time period total enrollment in Washington's public schools increased less than 5 percent. If other states experienced only half of Washington's growth in alternative education, the number of public alternative students grew from 3 million in 1981 to some 4 million, or nearly 7 percent of the public school population, in 1988.

While precise numbers are elusive, the existence of options within public education systems throughout the country is not. A substantial number of parents, students, and school districts have embraced the concept of choice and institutionalized it within public education. In 1987 71 percent of respondents answered yes to the question: "Do you think that parents in this community should or should not have the right to choose which local schools their children attend?" (Gallup & Clark, 1987, p. 20). This represented an increase of 4 percent from the previous year. A poll of Wisconsin residents by the Wisconsin Policy Research Institute in 1988 found that 75 percent of respondents believed that parents should have the right to choose a school or district for their children.

It is clear that options and choice within public education are here to stay and are growing substantially. It is also clear that the types of options have changed considerably during the last decade. What is the justification for public alternative education, and what are the characteristics of current public schools of choice? These topics are the focus of Chapter 2.

TWO

The Case for Public Alternative Education

WHY ARE ALTERNATIVES NEEDED?

Rationales for public alternative schools in the 1960s and 1970s were primarily ideological. Among the primary reasons given for supporting alternative education were choice, respect for the individual, and cultural pluralism.

Choice was presented as one of the distinguishing characteristics of a free society. A public education system without choice was appropriate for a totalitarian society but not for a democracy like ours. Richard Kammann's (1972) much-quoted passage reflected this reasoning:

> Imagine a town where every family is assigned arbitrarily to one local doctor by a ruling of the board of health. Imagine that the board of health assigns families only on the basis of the shortest distance from the home to the doctor's office. Imagine, finally, that when a family complains that the assigned doctor is not helping one of its ailing members, the board of health replies: "Sorry, no exception to doctor assignments." If this sounds like a totalitarian nightmare, it also is a description of the way school boards assign children to schools and teachers. (pp. 37–38)

Respect for the individual was a value to be encouraged within the classroom and outside the school. Teachers and parents were asked to consider the needs of their students and children. Allowing choice and options was a reflection of that respect. Haim Ginott (1973) endorsed this view:

> Give children choices. Offer them options. I remember talking with a group of teachers who were also parents, and one said, "You're telling me to give choices to my pupils. I don't even do that with my own children." I asked, "How old is your youngest?" She replied, "Two years." I said, "Can you say to him, 'Danny, would you like to have your eggs hard or very hard?'" She answered, "Well, I think I

could manage that." Then I asked her, "What difference does it make to Danny if you give him this kind of choice?" She concluded that Danny may say to himself, "My mother takes my wishes into account. I have something to say about my life. I am a person." (p. 20)

The civil rights movement, which contributed to the call for equity in the public schools, also led to the awakening of ethnic pride among minority groups. The traditional ideal of the melting pot gave way to the celebration of diversity in the minds of many Americans. The call for pluralism reached into the public schools and provided justification for creating options and alternatives. Neil Postman and Charles Weingartner (1971a), among others, articulated the case for pluralism:

A major characteristic of the American culture is that it is pluralistic. If pluralism means anything, it means the availability of options. Where there are no options, you have a fraudulent pluralism—the name without the reality. This is true in business, as well as in government. It is also true in education. (p. 12)

These rationales proved effective in generating emotional and intellectual support among educational reformers for alternative public schools, but more compelling reasons were needed to attract and sustain the support of the educational establishment and the general public. In 1974 the Panel on Youth of the President's Science Advisory Committee published its report, *Youth: Transition to Adulthood*. The report seriously questioned whether schools, especially the comprehensive high school, could meet the needs of all students. The authors observed:

Public expectations run high, asking schools and colleges to solve national problems of scientific preeminence, unemployables in the work force, disenchanted youth, social inequality, and even the breakdown of community. The functions seem almost endless, as these comprehensive institutions of mass preparation are pushed, and push themselves, to being all things to all young people. The problem is most acute when a single form, the public high school, attempts singlehandedly to meet the increasing spread of group demands and cultural tasks. But a variety of needs can only be met by a variety of institutions. (Panel on Youth . . . , 1974, p. 90)

Enrollment in secondary education had expanded dramatically during the first few decades of the twentieth century, as child labor laws took young people out of the workforce and compulsory attendance laws placed them in school until age 16. High schools responded with increased program offerings as opportunities outside the school disappeared. The prescription for filling the needs and occupying the interests of youth became one of more and more schooling, a prescription the President's Science Advisory Committee questioned:

> It appears reasonable now, however, to look a little more carefully at the task of becoming adult, to ask not the quantitative question, "How much more schooling?" but the qualitative one: "What are the appropriate environments in which youth can best grow into adults?" (Panel on Youth . . . , 1974, p. vii)

In response to its own question, the committee proposed a number of reforms for public schools. It recommended the formation of differentiated, or theme, schools and subunits, or schools within schools. These schools would offer choices among such specializations as music, physical education, science, arts, and so forth. The committee also recommended more integration of school and work by allowing students to spend part of the day outside the school in work settings. Additional recommendations included smaller schools, opportunities for public service, and educational vouchers.

Most of the committee's recommendations were neither new nor innovative. Since 1970 a number of states and more than a dozen national reports had called for the introduction of options into the public schools. In 1973 the National Commission on the Reform of Secondary Education recommended alternative paths to high school completion, credit for work experience, nonschool locations for learning, and the development of alternative schools and programs. In *The Education of Adolescents*, the U.S. Office of Education proposed "minischools, schools-without-walls, open schools, alternative schools, optimal programs, internships, parallel courses, independent study, free schools, and apprentice and action learning" (National Panel on High School and Adolescent Education, 1976, p. 5).

The failure of schools, particularly comprehensive high schools, to meet the needs and interests of a varied student body had been documented for some time. James Coleman's 1961 study, *The Adolescent Society*, portrayed a youth culture whose values were, in large part, antagonistic to those of the school. In the 1970s Coleman criticized schools' paternalistic treatment of youth while society was increasing its expectations for that group, and he wondered aloud whether America's youth had outgrown its schools. Phillip Cusick, in

Inside High School (1973), confirmed many of Coleman's observations, noting that school

> has systematically denied their involvement in basic, educational processes and relegated them to the position of watchers, waiters, order-followers, and passive receptacles for the depositing of disconnected bits of information. They, in turn, have rejected by paying only a minimal amount of forced attention to "formal" educational processes and simultaneously channeled their energy and enthusiasm into their groups wherein lie the more immediate rewards of activity, interest, and involvement. (p. 222)

Studies in the 1980s supported the observations made by Coleman and Cusick. Student interviews reported in Laurie Olsen and Melinda Moore's *Voices from the Classroom* (1982) revealed considerable dissatisfaction with teachers and classroom interactions. Students perceived the experiences to be boring and unpleasant. Ernest Boyer's *High School* (1983) and John Goodlad's *A Place Called School* (1984) found a sameness and narrowness in classroom instruction and content among schools that resulted in student passiveness and nonengagement. Secondary students surveyed in *A Place Called School* placed " 'teachers' and 'classes' far down the list in selecting 'the one best thing about this school' and placed 'friends' at the top" (p. 110).

Arthur Powell and colleagues concluded in *The Shopping Mall High School* (1985) that while comprehensive high schools served the academic top and bottom fairly well, the remaining 75 percent of students were treated as unspecial. They lacked the school advocates the special 25 percent of the students had. The unspecial received minimal counseling and attention. Their classes on the whole were larger than those of the special students, and teachers held lower expectations for the performance of unspecial students.

Recent conservative criticism directed toward public education, such as *A Nation at Risk* and other reports, has focused on the failure of schools to develop sufficient academic talent and to impart basic educational standards so that America may compete more effectively with other countries. Declining SAT scores, rising illiteracy and drop-out rates, and poor showings in international tests comparing American and foreign school-age children are presented as evidence of the failure of public education in this country.

The typical solution of these reports is to raise academic standards, increase graduation requirements, and make schools more competitive. The "get-tough" approach, while successful for motivating some students, is not successful for motivating others. The prescription of more of the same only harder has little appeal for students who were having academic difficulty before the reforms were in place.

In 1983, the Philadelphia school system developed a new promotion policy that abandoned social promotions and required mastery of a set of required skills for promotion. Implementation was postponed, however, when school officials discovered that 40 percent of the students would not have qualified for promotion under the new plan.

Liberal critics, such as William Glasser (1986), disagree with prescriptions that call for increased standards and requirements. He maintains such reforms lead only to more competition within the schools and inevitable hostility, disorder, and withdrawal from the 50 percent who have trouble competing. Glasser's concern about competition is shared by a number of school experts. Researchers at Johns Hopkins University Center for Social Organization of Schools have found that "A" and "B" students do well under the increased pressure but "D" and "F" students do not. According to the researchers, "such students have two real choices. They can drop out or endure three years of frustration and failure" (Schneider, 1986, p. 15). As Mary Metz (1986) has pointed out, much of the problem lies in the competitive nature of schools:

> Once students perform poorly in the academic sphere at school whether for reasons of cultural and social alienation or for any other reason, their school lives are likely to become painful and unrewarding. Schools are inherently competitive contexts which rank students according to their academic performance. . . . Because school is a competitive context, students can do well only in comparison to others who do poorly; high grades and honors have value because they are relatively rare. For those students whose poor performance serves to add lustre to the comparatively able performance of others, school offers few reasons for engagement, and many for resistance. For such students to maintain their pride, it may be necessary for them to make vivid to all around them their disdain for the academic enterprise. (p. 41)

More radical critics see competition as only one of the variables that affect student retention and motivation. Writers such as Michael Apple (1982), Henry Giroux (1983), and Peter McLaren (1989) describe a school culture that operates under structural constraints that reinforce the economic, racial, and sexual inequalities found in the larger society. Practices such as IQ testing, ability-group tracking, state mandated curricula, and local funding make schools into "company stores" that perpetuate social inequities. The relationship between school and society can be observed in the differentiated treatment of students that reflects their respective social and economic positions in society. As the National Coalition of Advocates for Children (1985) observed:

> Minority children do not matter as much as non-minority children judging by the disproportionate numbers of such children who are excluded and underserved by the schools. We know, for example, that black students are placed in classes for the mildly mentally handicapped at rates more than three times those of white children. Poor children, too, are considered less important than non-poor children, if we contrast the level of financing allocated for their education with that allocated for children in more affluent districts. Non-English speaking children still face language and cultural barriers throughout America, and in many places girls still encounter lower expectations than do boys. Differential treatment of children by race, sex, language, and handicap subverts our nation's deepest values of fairness. Such treatment also has enormous practical consequences. In fact, the failure to educate millions of children is turning the potential for social profit into grave deficit, the cost of which American taxpayers will bear both financially and socially, in terms of increased dependency and the loss of a sense of national purpose. (pp. viii-ix)

The dilemma facing schools is that on the one hand they are expected to provide all students with a basic education that allows them to be productive for their own self-satisfaction and for the economic betterment of society, while on the other hand they are expected to identify and cultivate academic talent among students who show potential in this area. This identification is done through competition, which necessarily produces losers as well as winners along the way. Success at competition, in turn, is affected by the relative economic, social, racial, and sexual advantages or disadvantages students bring with them to the schools. If radical critics are correct, schools do little to compensate for and, in fact, may accentuate the differences students bring with them.

Alternative schools and programs attempt to avoid the harmful effects of increased competition. Most options, excluding selective specialized schools, are noncompetitive. Student progress is typically measured by self-improvement and mastery rather than by comparison with others. Many of the options are ungraded. Students earn credit when work is completed at a level acceptable to the teacher. Students may take varying amounts of time to accomplish mastery and so progress at their own rates rather than the group's.

School success is defined more broadly in alternative schools and programs than in their conventional counterparts. Students may experience success in vocational, speciality theme, and experiential options within alternative education. Traditional schools are typically more limited in their view of school success. As Gary Wehlage and Robert Rutter (1986) have observed:

> A central problem with schools today is success is narrowly defined and restricted to a few at the top of their class ranking who are destined for college. . . . While proficiency in traditional academic subjects is important and serves to stimulate some youth, there are many more who should be encouraged to develop proficiency in other domains. (p. 391)

In addition to deemphasizing competition, many alternative schools provide a service-oriented curriculum to meet the special needs of their clientele. Daycare, parenting classes, support groups for substance and child abuse, self-esteem and life-skills classes are offered in conjunction with traditional academic classes. Alternative schools become part social agency to compensate students for disadvantages they may bring with them to school.

DROPOUT PREVENTION

Whether students are losing interest in schooling because of increased competition, inequality, dissatisfaction with their treatment by teachers and administrators, or uninteresting curricular fare, the undeniable fact remains that public education is not meeting the needs of a great many students. Nationally about 25 percent of students do not complete twelve years of schooling. In ten states the dropout rate exceeds 35 percent. In Philadelphia, Chicago, Detroit, New York, and Boston more than 40 percent of the students leave school before completion (Kunisawa, 1988). Dropout prevention and the concern for at-risk students became one of the top agenda items of educational reform in the late 1980s and a major factor behind the growth of public schools of choice.

The reasons for dropping out are many. In part, the answer is partly a matter of race and economics. But they do not tell the whole story. In Chicago, where the dropout rate is 50 percent, 57 percent of Hispanics, 56 percent of blacks, and 38 percent of whites drop out (Hahn, 1987). The dropout rate for *all* students is high. In Boston, where the dropout rate is 43 percent, black students make up 47 percent of the school population and 48 percent of the dropouts. White students are 29 percent of the school population and 28 percent of the dropouts. Hispanic students are 14 percent of the school population and 18 percent of the dropouts (Wheelock, 1986). It is not a problem found only among poor and minority students. It is a systematic failure affecting all ethnic and social groups.

Why do students drop out? A synthesis of research on the subject reported by Andrew Hahn (1987) reveals the following reasons for leaving school:

- Poor academic performance. Most dropouts have basic skills tests results in the bottom 20 percent of the population.
- Retention and suspension. Twenty-five percent of dropouts have been suspended from school.
- Attraction of work or military service.
- Learning disabilities and emotional problems.
- Language difficulties. Students with a primary language other than English are more likely to drop out.
- Pregnancy. Four out of five girls who become pregnant in high school drop out.
- Dislike of school.

From the categories above it is clear that academic difficulty is a primary reason for dropping out of school. Students who do not do well in school find it an unpleasant place to be and therefore leave. Increased academic standards and graduation requirements insure that schools will remain an unpleasant experience for many students. To the extent that academic performance is affected by innate abilities and the home environment of students, schools will find dropout prevention a very difficult goal to accomplish. There are areas, however, where schools can have an impact, as surveys of dropouts have revealed. A survey by Deborah Strother (1986) of Portland students who dropped out in 1980 revealed that 19 percent were dissatisfied with teachers, 15 percent disliked school in general, 13 percent disliked a specific school, 13 percent were bored or lacked interest in school, 12 percent were pregnant, 11 percent desired to attend an alternative school, and 17 percent had other reasons.

Student self-report data from the national High School and Beyond study yielded similar results. "Did not like school" and "poor grades" were the two main reasons school leavers gave for dropping out, both receiving a 35 percent response rate. At 15 percent and 10 percent respectively were "could not get along with teachers" and "expelled or suspended" (Ekstrom et al., 1986, p. 363).

Another analysis of the High School and Beyond data by Wehlage and Rutter (1986) found that students were more likely to drop out of a school where they felt that teachers were not interested in them and that school discipline was neither effective nor fair. According to Wehlage: "The act of rejecting an institution as fundamental to society as school must also be accompanied by the belief that the institution has rejected the person" (quoted in Wheelock, 1986, p. 8). In dropping out, students are expressing profound customer dissatisfaction with schools and their programs.

How to attract and maintain students has become a major challenge for public schools. It is a challenge that cannot be met by continuing to offer the comprehensive high school as the only educational option for secondary students. Increasingly communities have turned to alternative schools and programs to serve at-risk students. According to Hahn (1987): "Alternative schools are often the best available option for both potential and actual dropouts, especially if the programs employ reasonable criteria for eligibility, teach real skills, and accommodate working students" (p. 262).

In a number of cities, business leaders have called for the development of alternative schools and programs to combat the dropout rate. *The Portland Investment* (1987) outlines some of the school-business partnerships currently underway. One program is the Financial Services Academy, a school within a school option that provides practical training related to the financial services industry. Another program is the Partnership Project, a school-to-work transition option that provides at-risk high school students private-sector jobs and work-related classroom instruction. A third program is Vocational Village, a learning or resource center for students who have been unsuccessful in their home high schools. Training in seven career fields is available under one roof.

Philadelphia has established a magnet high school program called the Philadelphia High School Academy Association. The academies offer cooperative education options in electrical skills, automotive trades, business, and health. Employers provide paid work experience on job sites during the school year.

Atlanta's Archer High School offers a retail magnet program with support from a number of businesses including J.C. Penney, Neiman-

Marcus, Sears, Roebuck & Company, and the Georgia Retail Association. Dade County in Florida has instituted an Academy of Travel and Tourism located near the Miami International Airport. Students are prepared for careers in travel-related businesses.

New York City's Murry Bergtraum High School for Business Careers is a partnership between the public schools and the city's financial community. Students concentrate in one of three areas in banking and finance and participate in paid internship programs. In addition to this program, numerous other options are available for at-risk students in the city's schools.

Not only business leaders at the local level but politicians at the state level have called for increased choice and options in public education. The National Governors' Association (1986) proposed "an idea in the great American tradition: that you can increase excellence by increasing choice" (p. 67). The report endorsed state programs that allow students to attend school districts outside their home district.

Examples of these are Colorado's "second chance" option, which allows high school students who have not succeeded in their home school district to transfer to another, and Washington's and Oregon's provision that permits dropouts to enroll in private alternative schools with state approval at state expense.

Arkansas, Minnesota, and Nebraska have moved beyond "second chance" opportunities for unsuccessful students and adopted open enrollment plans to allow parental choice among public schools in those states. In Iowa families are allowed to send their children to adjacent districts if a different program is available. In Arkansas, Minnesota, and Nebraska students may choose schools across district lines if there is room and desegregation efforts are not upset. Arizona, Colorado, Florida, Iowa, Maine, Minnesota, Oregon, and Rhode Island allow high school students to take courses at post secondary institutions and receive credit at state expense.

The argument for alternative education to assist in dropout prevention is primarily one of national self-interest. Underskilled and unemployed adults are an economic burden to society. However, the question of equity should also weight heavily when considering reasons for providing options for at-risk youth. As one national report observed: "Society spends up to ten times as much on advantaged kids as it does for the disadvantaged. Why not partially equalize this and give the dropouts an opportunity to be educated in an alternative setting" (Education Commission of the States, 1986, p. 7).

The question of equity looms large in the future of public education for our country. Demographic data indicate students will increasingly be drawn from poor and minority homes. Currently, 25 percent of all students live in poverty. By the year 2000 the percentage is expected to be near 33 percent. Currently 29 percent of all students are nonwhite. By the year 2000 the percentage is expected to be almost 35 percent (Haberman, 1988). This trend, combined with the knowledge that school performance is influenced by social and economic class, means a continuing and increasing market for options in public education.

DECLINING ENROLLMENTS

K–12 enrollment in public education declined almost 15 percent between 1971 and 1984. Elementary enrollment has been gradually rising since 1985, but secondary enrollment continues to fall and is not expected to increase until 1992.

Declining enrollments represent not only a loss of students for public schools but also a loss of dollars. Virtually every state reimburses local school districts for the number of students they enroll. Attendance figures taken in the fall are the basis for determining enrollment and the subsequent state reimbursement. The percentage of that reimbursement varies from state to state. In New Hampshire the state pays local districts 5 percent of the cost of educating a student. In Hawaii the state pays 90 percent. The national average is around 50 percent. In 1985–86 the average state per pupil expenditure was $3,752 (Digest of Educational Statistics, 1988). An average district receiving 50 percent state reimbursement whose enrollment declines by just 40 students loses $74,100 in state revenue.

The loss of revenue has prompted local districts to reconsider their attitudes toward at-risk and truant students. In the past these students were at best tolerated and at worst encouraged to leave so that the education of the remaining students could be carried on smoothly. Now local districts are courting at-risk and recruiting truant students aggressively, establishing alternative schools and programs to meet their needs and hold their interest. It is fair to say the growth of alternative schools in the 1980s was in part attributable to the self-interest of local school districts. As Wehlage observed: "Schools can generate income they would not otherwise have by preventing students from dropping out or by persuading former dropouts to return. A good program for marginal students can make money for a school" (Wehlage, 1983, p. 17).

The operation of alternative schools and programs, excluding magnet schools, can be a relatively inexpensive undertaking. Respondents to Raywid's (1982) 1981 national survey indicated that 62 percent spent the same or less on per pupil expenses as other schools in their district. The 1988 survey of Washington's public alternative schools and programs by the author found the percentage in that state to be 77 percent (Young, 1988).

Students in alternative schools are frequently allowed to take coursework and to use facilities, such as gyms, libraries, athletic fields, and vocational equipment, at the traditional school. This sharing of plant, materials, and teachers means complete duplication is not always necessary when an educational option is put into place. As Wehlage (1983) indicated, some school districts find they can even turn a small profit by establishing alternative schools and programs. While it would be unfair to conclude that the primary motive for supporting options in public schools is economic, it would be naive to pretend that economics play no part in the process.

DESEGREGATION

In 1970 white children made up 75 percent of K–12 enrollment in the nation's largest metropolitan school districts. By 1984 that percentage had fallen to 30 percent. Today, minority enrollment in the nation's fifteen largest school districts ranges from 70 percent to 96 percent (Kellogg, 1988). White flight from America's cities has proven to be an extremely difficult trend to halt or reverse. The impetus for it can be traced back to federal court decisions in the early 1970s that required the desegregation of urban school systems.

The initial remedy to segregated school systems was forced busing, which resulted in tension and conflict and accelerated white flight from urban schools. An alternative to busing was the introduction of magnet schools in the mid-1970s. As discussed in Chapter 1, magnet schools are schools with special curricula and resources designed to make them so attractive that students from all racial and ethnic backgrounds will want to attend them. Most magnet schools feature a theme or specialized program of study, such as performing arts, math/science, multicultural education, humanities, and careers of various kinds.

Most magnet schools are not selective in their admission requirements. While some magnet schools do have strict admission requirements based on grades, test scores, or grade-point average, they constitute about 33 percent of the total number. Race, however, is a criterion for admission to all magnet programs. Designed primarily for desegregation, magnet schools try to achieve a racial balance reflective of the city school system. This can result in students being turned away because of their race. For example, in 1986–87 nine of the twelve magnet high schools in St. Louis had vacancies but had to turn away black students because of underenrollment by whites. In Los Angeles, where 26,000 students attended eighty-six magnet schools in 1989, seats for Anglo students went unfilled in inner-city magnets while magnets in Anglo areas were swamped with requests.

Magnet schools have had mixed success in attracting white students and desegregating school systems. Most cities have been unable to meet court-mandated goals for racial diversity in their schools. In cities with extremely large minority school-age populations, desegregation is no longer a viable goal. What magnet schools have done, however, is to slow down white flight and in some cases reverse it. In the Georgetown area of Washington, D. C., a magnet school complex of six schools increased public school enrollment from 11 percent of all school-age children in 1980 to 63 percent in 1987 (Jones, 1988). Prince George's County, Maryland, has managed to attract 3,000 students previously enrolled in private schools since instituting magnet schools in 1985. Buffalo has had similar success in attracting parochial and private school students back into the public education system (Snider, 1987).

Not everyone is happy with magnet schools, however. First, there is the question of cost. Best estimates indicate that magnet schools cost between 10 to 12 percent more to operate than traditional schools. Second, there is the problem of siphoning off the best students from neighborhood schools. With few positive role models left behind, neighborhood schools decline in quality even more and are perceived as second-class institutions by those students and teachers who remain. Third, there is the question of equity. Some magnet schools do have entrance requirements, which necessarily favor those students who have the academic preparation and support from home to score well on entrance examinations. Should they be receiving a more expensive education than those who fail to qualify for such programs? Should students attending even nonselective magnet schools benefit from a more expensive education than those in neighborhood schools?

These are difficult questions to answer. Some school districts have responded to the problem of equity by turning most or all of their schools into magnets. New York's East Harlem transformed all of its middle and junior high schools into magnet programs. Cambridge, Massachusetts, eliminated all of its K–8 neighborhood schools and made each one into a magnet school: Parents must select their top three preferences from among the district's thirteen elementary schools. This approach represents a controlled choice for parents and is gaining popularity among urban school districts. Seattle and Boston began undertaking their own versions of controlled choice during the 1989–90 school year. A more dramatic response to the question of equity is to do what Montclair, New Jersey, and Richmond, California have done. Both cities made virtually all of their schools magnets.

While magnet schools are an imperfect response to desegregation and related problems in America's urban school system, they appear to have more positive results than negative. Perhaps the primary reason for supporting magnet schools is that they offer minority children excellent educational programs, which in the past have been available only to children who could afford private school tuition or a home in an affluent suburban community.

EDUCATIONAL RESEARCH AND DEVELOPMENT

Alternative schools and programs serve as an ideal research and development arm of public education. Because of their smaller size and greater autonomy and flexibility, they are more easily adaptable to experimental designs. Conducting research in traditional schools, especially large ones, can be difficult because of standardization of programs and practices. Teacher assignments, class schedules, and curricular content are usually fixed and not easily changed. It is also the case in most traditional schools that administrators are less willing to allow experimentation with programs that serve "more able" students than with programs that serve the "less able." The more academic a program is perceived to be, the less tolerance there is for change and risk taking regarding it. This attitude is, in part, a response to the more vocal demands for accountability from parents of the "more able" children.

Within alternative schools and programs there is frequently greater tolerance of research and experimentation. Many options began as experiments themselves, and a positive attitude toward change remains. Today, public schools of choice are more active in educational experimentation than their conventional counterparts.

Learning styles, flexible scheduling, team teaching, cooperative and community-based learning, individualized instruction, mentoring, and behavioral modification techniques can be found in practice.

Because of the focus on the whole student, opportunities exist for research in affective as well as cognitive education. The areas of self-esteem and interpersonal relationships have historically been ones of major emphasis in alternative schools and programs, and, as we shall see in Chapter 3, the emphasis on affective education is a key ingredient in the effectiveness of these schools and programs.

Schools of choice are often on the cutting edge of the social issues that confront public education. Substance abuse is a primary example. This social issue was the focus of a number of alternative schools and programs long before it became fashionable to include it in conventional public schools. Other topics with a long history of involvement in schools of choice include vandalism, child abuse, assertiveness training, teenage pregnancy, and daycare.

While the potential for public alternative schools and programs to make positive contributions to educational innovation and improvement appears great, what evidence exists to indicate they will? How effective are public schools of choice? Are they successful in improving student attitudes and achievement? Do they provide useful models for educational reform? These and other questions will be the focus of the next chapter, as the research on public alternative schools and programs is reviewed.

THREE

How Effective Are Public Alternative Schools?

EARLY RESEARCH ON PUBLIC ALTERNATIVE EDUCATION

The popularity of public alternative education in the 1970s generated considerable research on the effectiveness of various schools and programs. As the newness wore off and the popularity of alternative education subsided, so did research on the subject. Since 1980 the number of published studies on the effectiveness of public schools of choice have been relatively few. As a result, some of the research base for alternative education has remained dependent on studies conducted during the 1970s. Reliance on earlier research presents some problems, however. Early evaluations of alternative schools and programs were characterized by weak research design and inadequate data collection. As a result, conclusions about the effectiveness of these programs are, at best, tenuous.

In a research review of nineteen program evaluations conducted in the 1970s, Daniel Duke and Irene Muzio (1978) attempted to answer the question, "How well do alternative schools educate students?" Their conclusion: "Data contained in the nineteen evaluations and reports we reviewed do not permit us to answer this question with any degree of confidence. . . . We only hope that the quality of the evaluations does not reflect the quality of the programs being evaluated" (pp. 481–483). The authors listed a number of weaknesses in the evaluations they reviewed. The most glaring included:

- Lack of a control or comparison group
- Poor record keeping
- No randomized sample of students, teachers, and parents
- Failure to report data on program dropouts
- Lack of pre- and posttest comparison
- Lack of follow-up on dropouts and early graduates of programs

- Tendency to apologize for or offer impressionistic data concerning negative results

Most research studies on alternative education conducted by independent investigators in the 1970s relied on data generated by the schools and programs themselves and are of questionable value for the reasons listed above. Since 1980 more rigorous studies have been conducted using data generated by independent investigators. A review of these studies follows.

RECENT RESEARCH ON PUBLIC ALTERNATIVE SCHOOLS

The extent and variety of public schools of choice were surveyed by Mary Ann Raywid (1982). She contacted 2,500 secondary alternative schools and programs, most of them nonmagnets, in 1981. Twelve hundred of the schools responded to the survey. The survey collected information on the types and distribution of options around the country, which was described in Chapter 2. In addition to that information, the survey revealed that the following qualities characterized these schools and programs:

- High staff morale; 90 percent of teachers felt strong ownership of their programs.
- Increased student attendance; 81 percent of schools reported student attendance had increased or greatly increased compared to patterns at previous schools.
- Good student-teacher relationships; 63 percent of the schools identified student-teacher interaction as their most distinctive feature.
- Smallness; 69 percent of the schools had fewer than 200 students.
- Choice; 79 percent of the students were there by choice.

Raywid's study was primarily a descriptive one. Except for data on attendance and teacher morale, no attempt was made to evaluate the effectiveness of the schools in improving student attitudes or achievement. Conclusions in these areas cannot be drawn.

A U.S. Department of Education Study undertaken by Patricia Fleming and colleagues (1982) examined more than 1,000 magnet schools and found them to have fewer student behavior problems and higher teacher satisfaction than conventional public schools. Researchers also found greater teacher and student commitment in magnet than in conventional schools. A more detailed study of forty-five magnet schools in fifteen urban districts by Rolf Blank in 1984 concluded that magnet schools provide high-quality education. One-third of the schools were rated high in every category, and more than one-half were rated high in most categories as identified by the researchers. The categories included (1) having a special curricular theme or method of instruction, (2) playing a unique role in desegregation within its district, (3) relying on voluntary enrollment, and (4) offering open access to students beyond a regular attendance zone (Blank, 1984). Magnet schools were also successful in promoting high student achievement. Eighty percent of magnet students had achievement scores in reading and math that were above the average for their respective districts.

Another study of forty-one magnet schools in eight school districts was conducted by the New York State Education Department (1985). It found that magnet schools significantly improved student achievement and attendance and lowered dropout rates. A majority of the forty-one schools had higher achievement scores than their district averages. Ninety-eight percent of the magnets had higher attendance, and three-quarters had lower dropout rates than their district averages.

Different by Design by Mary Metz (1986) was a yearlong study of three magnet schools located in one district. She found that innovations in the magnet schools made it easier to work with students from diverse backgrounds and with those who had academic and social difficulties. According to Metz, "The magnet schools could and did serve the less privileged children of the city well" (p. 210).

The ability of magnet schools to demonstrate academic effectiveness with both able and less able students has enhanced their attractiveness as an educational option. Results such as those mentioned above have led observers like Dennis Doyle and Marsha Levine (1984) to conclude that neighborhood schools no longer make sense. They see magnet schools, particularly in urban areas, as powerful tools for educational change: "Magnet schools offer a strategy for low-cost, highly visible, incremental change that could conceivably transform American education" (p. 270).

The relationship of student and teacher attitudes to alternative and conventional schools was analyzed by Gerald Smith, Thomas Gregory, and Richard Pugh (1981). The authors chose seven alternative and six conventional high schools for comparison. While the thirteen schools were not systematically matched, they were all judged as good or very good by most educators and were a source of pride in their respective communities.

A nonrandomized sample of 459 alternative high school students and 104 of their teachers, along with 622 conventional high school students and 379 of their teachers, were administered the Statements About Schools Inventory (SAS). Designed specifically for the study, the SAS contains four scales corresponding to the top four levels of Maslow's hierarchy of needs: security, social needs, esteem, and self-actualization.

Security needs included a stable, orderly, and controlled environment. A high score on the scale indicated an environment that was controlled and ordered without being oppressive. A low score indicated an environment with little emphasis on control and order. Social needs represented the opportunity to establish friendships with students and teachers and belong to a group. A high score on the scale indicated an environment that emphasized social relationships and feelings of belonging to a group. A low score indicated an environment not committed to socializing. Esteem needs involved feelings of success and capability. A high score reflected an environment that fostered many paths to success and reduced those to failure. A low score reflected an environment that did not emphasize success. Self-actualization needs represented individuals' growth in becoming more complete and self-satisfied. A high score indicated an environment that fostered personal growth. A low score indicated an environment less committed to personal growth.

Results of the SAS administration were dramatic. Students and teachers in the alternative schools scored significantly higher than their conventional counterparts in the areas of social, esteem, and self-actualization needs. They also scored higher, but not significantly higher, in security needs. What was impressive is that the lowest-scoring alternative school had significantly higher scores than the highest-scoring conventional school. The authors speculated that choice was the reason for the dramatic showing of the alternative schools. In their words: "Common sense leads one to conclude that individuals are more likely to value and see merit in programs they elect to attend than in those imposed upon them" (Smith et al., 1981, p. 564).

The academic achievement and attitudes of elementary alternative and conventional students were compared in a Rand Corporation work, *A Study of Alternatives in American Education* (1981). Data were collected over a three-year period from the Alum Rock Voucher Demonstration Project. Student reading scores and attitude responses about self and peers attending alternative and conventional schools were analyzed. No significant differences were found at the school level. At the classroom level, though, "reading achievement was higher in classes whose teachers saw themselves as more autonomous and influential than their colleagues" (*A Study of Alternatives. . . . ,* 1981, p. 54). Researchers advised caution in interpreting their results, however:

> The student achievement data available for those years were flawed by test administration problems; and non-cognitive measures were administered only to small, and potentially unrepresentative, subsamples of students. Further, because of the nature of parent and teacher (school) choices, students, and classes could not be randomly assigned to regular and alternative schools. (p. 51)

Given the shortcomings of the study, one is left wondering about its usefulness.

Academic achievement as well as the attitudes of delinquent students attending alternative and conventional schools were analyzed by Martin Gold and David Mann (1984) in *Expelled to a Friendlier Place.* The authors compared approximately sixty at-risk students from three alternative secondary schools with a matched group of students from conventional secondary schools in the same districts. Alternative and conventional students were matched by age, sex, grade-point average, discipline history, self-esteem, and attitude toward school. Pre- and posttest results over the school year were the basis for comparison. The study yielded the following results:

- Alternative students were significantly less disruptive in school at the end of the study than conventional students.
- Teachers rated alternative students who returned to conventional schools as slightly better behaved than conventional students.
- Alternative students were significantly more positive about school and confident in their role as students than conventional students.
- While alternative students received slightly improved grades when they reenrolled in conventional schools, their achievement test scores did not improve and were not different from those of conventional students.

In attempting to understand the meaning of these results the authors focused on the importance of perceived flexibility of school rules and academic prospects. Students who were positive about school and confident in their role as students perceived their schools as flexible whether they were alternative or conventional schools.

The perception of flexibility existed when students felt teachers took into consideration their feelings, needs, and abilities when teaching. Alternative schools were more likely to be perceived as flexible than conventional schools. Alternative students reported more personal contacts with teachers and classmates. Classroom observations by researchers using low-inference observation instruments revealed more praise and acknowledgment of students in alternative than in conventional schools.

Student achievement and attendance were the focus of two studies by Eileen Foley: one with Susan McConnaughy in 1982, *Towards School Improvement,* and another with Peggy Crull in 1984, *Educating the At-Risk Student.* Both studies dealt with the progress of approximately 300 students who attended eight alternative high schools. The schools were designed to serve at-risk students with poor attendance and underachievement. The 1982 study evaluated the students at the end of their first semester at the alternative schools. The 1984 study evaluated them at the end of their fourth semester at the schools.

Results from the two studies indicated that the alternative programs cut student absences by 40 percent and increased credits earned by 60 percent. These figures represented a significant improvement over students' previous performance at their conventional high schools.

While attendance and credits earned improved significantly, projected graduation rates did not. Many of the students entered the alternative schools at an advanced age and with few earned credits. As a result only about one-half of the students were projected to complete the necessary graduation requirements by age 21. Still, the authors remained optimistic, given the dramatic improvement that occurred in the alternative schools. Among the authors' suggestions were providing alternatives at an earlier age for at-risk students, ideally immediately after junior high. This would reduce the number of students falling so drastically far behind in credit accumulation.

The relationship of the culture of alternative and conventional schools to student attitudes was explored by Thomas Gregory and Gerald Smith (1987) in *High Schools as Communities.* Gregory and Smith compared a small (175 students, 12 teachers) alternative high school with a large (1,000 students, 70 teachers) conventional high school located in the same community. Data were collected from 446 students and 124 teachers using the SAS inventory and through individual and small group interviews of selected teachers and students.

The authors found a number of differences between the alternative school, which they dubbed "Lilliput," and the conventional school, which they called "Gulliver." The first difference was that teachers and students at Lilliput shared similar values and a common educational philosophy. Focus on goals and commitment to them was easier than at Gulliver, where a much broader set of values and greater number of educational philosophies existed. Cliques thrived at Gulliver, as students subdivided into groups based on interests, ability, and social status. At Lilliput such distinctions were not found.

Second, student and teacher roles were less distinct and separate at Lilliput than at Gulliver. Students and teachers were on a first-name basis. Out-of-class activities such as picnics, fieldtrips, and overnights were frequently undertaken. Students were encouraged to bring both personal and academic concerns to teachers. Small-group advisory sections were scheduled monthly to discuss nonacademic matters.

Third, unlike the situation at Gulliver, where the prescribed curriculum was the ultimate consideration, Lilliput allowed for greater instructional flexibility. The textbook was less likely to be the only source of information as teachers attempted to relate subject matter to students' needs and interests. Programs of individual study were available when students wanted to go beyond regularly scheduled courses. Students were even allowed to teach occasional courses.

Fourth, discipline at Gulliver focused on control, and control was seen as being external. The student body was considered a security problem. At Lilliput teachers attempted to foster self-control in their students. Mistakes were allowed, and a greater level of trust between teachers and students existed.

Because of its size, Lilliput was able to develop a sense of community. By sense of community the authors meant "the degree to which all its inhabitants see themselves as one group that collaborates to make the school work" (Gregory & Smith, 1987, p. 50). This reduction in size and development of a sense of community resulted in a number of positive characteristics at Lilliput:

- A heightened sense of efficacy for students and teachers
- A principal as head teacher, allowing the removal of the authority barrier between the principal and the rest of the faculty
- A support system for teachers
- A democratic governance model
- An end to control as a primary issue
- Easier identification of teachers and students with the school

While Gregory and Smith did not report the results of the SAS Inventory for Lilliput and Gulliver, they did report state evaluation scores in a number of areas for the two schools. While Lilliput and Gulliver were virtually identical in achievement test scores, Lilliput ranked higher in self-esteem, understanding others, interest in school, societal responsibility, and appreciation of human accomplishments. Care must be taken in drawing conclusions from this study, since the two schools were not matched on the basis of socioeconomic status, ethnicity, or academic achievement. But when these results are combined with those from the other studies, some generalizations about the effectiveness of alternative schools and programs can be made with a modest degree of confidence.

First, it appears that students in alternative schools have more positive attitudes about themselves and about school than similar students attending conventional schools. Results from Fleming and colleagues (1982), Smith and colleagues (1981), Gold and Mann (1984), and Gregory and Smith (1987) support this conclusion. The Rand study (*A Study of Alternatives* . . . , 1981) found no significant differences in the attitudes of conventional and alternative students, but its reliability is questionable because of numerous research design weaknesses.

Second, it appears that alternative schools help to improve student attendance and lead to better in-school behavior. Fleming and colleagues (1982), Raywid (1982), Gold and Mann (1984), Foley and McConnaughy (1982), Foley and Crull (1984), and the New York State Education Department (1985) study provide the support for this conclusion.

Third, participation in alternative schools and programs has been shown to be related to higher academic achievement. Blank (1984) and the New York State Education Department (1985) found this to be true for magnet schools. Gold and Mann (1984) found attendance in alternative schools to result in slightly better grades but not in increased test scores. The two studies by Foley (Foley & Crull, 1984; Foley & McConnaughy, 1982) indicated that earned credits increased significantly with participation in alternative schools. The Rand study (*A Study of Alternatives* . . . , 1981) found no significant difference in reading test scores between alternative and conventional schools.

It is obvious from this short review that the research base on which these generalizations rest is not large. As indicated at the beginning of the chapter, the number of recently published studies on the effectiveness of public schools of choice is quite small. It is clear an urgent need exists for additional research on alternative schools and programs, particularly in the area of academic achievement.

CHARACTERISTICS OF EFFECTIVE PUBLIC ALTERNATIVE SCHOOLS

A review of these studies does provide some insight to the characteristics of effective alternative schools and programs. In her two studies Foley described the characteristics that made the eight alternative schools effective. They were:

- Positive student-teacher relationships. Students could talk about nonacademic as well as academic subject matter with teachers.
- Student-centered curriculum. Instruction was related to students' personal experiences.
- Varied roles for teachers. Teachers served as advisors, attendance officers, and guidance counselors to meet a variety of student needs.
- Noncompetitive classrooms. Peer cooperation and sharing were emphasized. Positive relationships among students were encouraged.
- Clear mission. Schools targeted their students and tailored programs to fit their needs.
- School size. Schools were small enough to allow students to feel part of a group, yet large enough to provide necessary resources.

These ingredients as well as some others were identified in a study of six effective alternative schools by Gary Wehlage (1983). Among the characteristics of effective schools listed by Wehlage were:

- Smallness. Enrollments in the six schools ranged from twenty-five to sixty.
- Program autonomy. Teachers were given latitude and responsibility for admission, dismissal, course offerings, and credit arrangements.
- Empowerment. Teachers were given a sense of program ownership.
- Teacher optimism. Teachers assumed they could be successful with students. They saw their role as dealing with the whole

student, which extended to activities outside the classroom
and material outside the regular curriculum.
- Family atmosphere. Students felt comfortable in a supportive
  peer and adult environment. Cooperation rather than competition characterized learning experiences.
- Experiential curriculum. There were opportunities to have
  learning experiences outside school through voluntary service,
  internships, or job placements.

Smallness, concern for the whole student, supportive environment, and sense of community/clear mission are the key ingredients
of effective alternative schools and programs. What is interesting is
that these characteristics have been identified as key ingredients not
only in effective public schools of choice but also in effective private
schools and businesses.

Smallness

Gregory and Smith's (1987) study noted the effects school size
had on student attitudes and school culture within Lilliput and Gulliver. Development of a sense of community, informal relationships,
and commitment to common goals and philosophy were facilitated by
the smallness of the former. More formal relationships, lack of consensus on educational goals and philosophy, existence of cliques
among students, and concern for order and security resulted from the
largeness of the latter.

The qualities observed by Gold and Mann (1984) in effective alternative schools—flexibility, personal contacts, and consideration of
student needs—are also influenced by school size. It is easier to be
flexible, achieve a feeling of intimacy, and attend to individual needs
when the scale of operation is small. A number of studies have indicated that students in smaller schools experience benefits that derive
directly from the size of their schools.

Roger Barker and Paul Gump (1964) in their classic work, *Big
School, Small School*, found that students in smaller schools participated in extracurricular activities and held positions of importance
and responsibility in greater proportion than students in larger
schools. Students in small schools gained satisfaction and confidence
from participating and developing confidence in group action, while
students in large schools gained satisfaction vicariously by learning
about school affairs. The authors concluded:

> Our findings and theory posit a negative relationship between school size and individual student participation. What seems to happen is that as schools get larger and settings inevitably become more heavily populated, more of the students are less needed; they become superfluous, redundant. (1964, p. 202)

Barker and Gump's results are supported by a number of researchers (e.g., Coleman, 1981; Garbarino, 1980; Grabe, 1976; Ianni, 1979; Lindsay, 1982, 1984). Mark Grabe (1976) found greater student participation in extracurricular activities in small schools, which, in turn, influenced student self-esteem. Paul Lindsay's 1982 study found that small school size increased student participation as well as student satisfaction and attendance. Results from Lindsay's 1984 study indicated that students from small schools experienced greater participation in extracurricular activities than students in large schools, which, in turn, had a positive effect on later participation in social activities as young adults. Francis Ianni and Elizabeth Reuss-Ianni (1979) concluded that large schools encouraged violence and disruption, and James Garbarino (1980) observed that large schools contributed to adolescent crime.

The size of schools also may have an effect on students' academic performance. Peter Mortimore and colleagues (1988) reported the results of a large-scale study of 2,000 students in fifty English elementary schools. They found middle- to small-sized schools (160 or fewer students) to be positively related to students' cognitive outcomes. James Coleman identified increasing size and the bureaucratization of the school as a major problem in public education and one of the reasons for parent attraction to private schools. In the conventional school, he observed:

> The exercising of authority—regarded as humane and fair when the teacher knows the students and the parents well—comes to be regarded as inhumane and unfair when it is impersonally administered by a school staff member (teacher or otherwise) who hardly knows the student and seldom sees the parents. (1981, p. 162)

While some parents patronize private education to provide their children with a better academic experience, many choose private education because they want the school and its teachers to take an active interest in their children. Private schools tend to be small and limited in enrollment, so that attending to students' needs and interests is feasible. Large public schools, like the comprehensive high school, by virtue of their size and enrollment, can often be impersonal and inattentive to individual student needs. Some students "fall between the cracks," become lost, and drop out.

Concern for the Whole Student

Concern for the whole student is reflected in Gold and Mann's (1984) conclusion about the importance of students' perceiving a school as flexible and teachers as taking students' feelings, needs, and abilities into consideration. Wehlage's (1983) characteristic of teacher optimism and Foley's (1982, 1984) characteristics of positive student-teacher relationship and student-centered curriculum are also examples of concern for the student. Optimistic teachers are interested in the whole student and assume responsibility for their success. They are also willing to engage students in informal and out-of-class activities, as Gregory and Smith (1987) observed at Lilliput. Teachers who are positive and student-centered attempt to make their instruction relevant to student needs and experiences and are willing to discuss both nonacademic as well as academic subjects with students.

Arthur Powell and colleagues (1985) observed that a concern for the whole student was one of the distinguishing characteristics separating conventional public and effective private schools. To illustrate the point, they reported that a student who had attended both private and public schools commented that "Teachers . . . would 'rush to help you' in the private school if you were not doing well—'that was part of their job.' Teachers in the public schools would help too, of course, but you had to reach out to them" (p. 215). Powell observed that private school teachers were expected to counsel and advise students as well as teach them. In the words of one public school teacher, the most significant difference between a public and private school was "that teachers in the latter 'are being paid to know your kid' " (p. 216). Raywid's (1982) survey result that alternative schools identified student-teacher interaction as their most distinctive feature is further evidence of the concern for the whole student by public schools of choice.

Supportive Environment

As noted in Chapter 2, increased competition results in increasing numbers of losers who can either absorb their failure or drop out.

The studies by Wehlage (1983) and Foley (1982, 1984) indicate that alternative schools are more effective when they encourage a family atmosphere that supports cooperation rather than competition. While the schools studied by Wehlage and Foley served at-risk students, cooperative approaches to learning can benefit all students.

The cooperative learning approach has gained a great deal of attention and support over the last ten to fifteen years. It involves grouping and instructional strategies that place responsibility on the shoulders of several students rather than on a single individual. Cooperative learning begins with a teacher-assigned heterogeneous group of three to five students. The group is responsible for completing a task that requires both individual and group skills. Teacher evaluation of the completed task is based on both individual and group performance. Considerable research has been conducted to analyze the outcomes of cooperative learning in the classroom, and the results have been overwhelmingly positive. Robert Slavin (1983) and David and Roger Johnson (1987) have conducted extensive research on cooperative learning and found it to be significantly related to increased academic achievement and improved student relationships within the classroom.

Sense of Community/Clear Mission

A sense of community and a commitment to shared values are, according to Gregory and Smith (1987), the major reasons for the success of Lilliput. Because of this sense and this commitment students and staff were better able to collaborate and act effectively to make the school work. A shared philosophy was possible because Lilliput had a sense of what it stood for.

Foley (1982, 1984) identified a clear mission as an important characteristic of the effective alternative schools she studied. The successful alternative schools had a sense of purpose. They knew their student population and designed specific programs to meet their needs. Unlike the conventional public schools, which must be all things to all students, the alternative schools concentrated on what they did best. Designing different programs for specific student populations makes both pedagogical and organizational sense according to Dennis Doyle and Marsha Levine (1984): "Learning demands an intellectual engagement between student and teacher that is more easily achieved if both parties know why they are there" (p. 269).

A clear mission and sense of community facilitate agreement among staff and students about the direction of a school, which, in turn, contributes to increased school or program effectiveness. Effectiveness in the typical conventional school is more difficult because it must serve a much larger and heterogeneous clientele. It cannot concentrate resources and effort on any one particular group of students for fear of alienating the rest. Therefore, its response is to offer a little something for everyone, thus pleasing but offending no on. A sense of community and clear mission are important characteristics of effective private schools and businesses, as well as public schools of choice. According to Donald Erickson (1982), much of the success of private schools is due to "that kind of cohesive community or 'fellowship' that exists when people are held together by mutual commitment to common purpose and to each other, by a sense of doing something special, and by consensus about the goals to be achieved" (p. 8).

CONCLUSIONS

These characteristics of effective public alternative schools and programs are found not only in the research on private schools but in the literature on effective businesses. Thomas Peters and Robert Waterman, in their bestseller, *In Search of Excellence* (1983), identified eight characteristics of effective businesses:

1. A bias for action: a willingness to experiment, innovate, do something;
2. Closeness to the customer: listening to and caring about the needs of the customer;
3. Autonomy and entrepreneurship: encouraging independent decision making and risk taking;
4. Productivity through people: treating employees with respect, rewarding them appropriately;
5. Hands-on, value-driven character: standing for a common purpose, having a shared set of values;
6. Sticking to the knitting: specializing in what you do best;
7. Simple form, lean staff: remaining simple in organization—small is beautiful;
8. Simultaneous loose-tight properties: allowing autonomy within a central direction.

From our review of the literature we can see that most, if not all, of these characteristics are found in alternative schools and programs.

1. Public schools of choice typically demonstrate a willingness to innovate and experiment. They are frequently on the cutting edge of educational issues and change.
2. They are close to their customers (students), attending to a variety of academic and nonacademic needs through a concern for the whole student.
3. Their smallness allows greater program autonomy and decision making than is the case in most conventional schools.
4. Treating students with respect, emphasizing group cooperation rather than individual competition, and rewarding appropriately are hallmarks of public schools of choice. Student success is not dependent on the failure of others.
5. The smallness of schools of choice facilitates a common set of shared values and goals among students and staff. These schools stand for something.
6. By not being all things to all people, schools of choice can specialize in and concentrate on what they do well. The student clientele served and curriculum offered are frequently limited, allowing the school to focus on the most important and immediate needs of students.
7. Small is beautiful, and most public schools of choice are typically small. They operate with a simple organization and lean staff (sometimes too lean).
8. Finally, although they operate within the guidelines of the central administration, they are able to exercise some individual autonomy. Sometimes that autonomy is the result of neglect by the central administration. More often, however, it is the recognition of expertise and effectiveness.

Testimony of the relationship between effective schools of choice and effective businesses comes from *Time For Results* (National Governors' Association, 1986). In this report the nation's governors noted

> Experience with public alternative schools shows that many have the distinct shared philosophy, mission, and faculty agreement called for in literature on effective schools. Indeed, many outstanding schools share certain characteristics of effective corporations. One of the similarities is clear, distinct, focused mission. When schools are permitted to develop some specialization, their effectiveness increases. (p. 69)

As the report indicates, there is much to learn from public alternative education. The call for a "clear, distinct, focused mission" from our schools is one we hear a great deal about today. Conventional public schools, especially the comprehensive high school, are seen by many as having no focused mission. In the attempt to be all things to all students they have come to stand for nothing. What public alternative education offers is an array of specialized options, each with a clear, distinct, and focused mission and each with the necessary shared commitment to a set of values to provide success.

How do alternative schools achieve this commitment and focus? In Chapter 4 we will examine some of these specialized options when we visit six exemplary public schools of choice and learn what makes them effective yet distinct from one another.

FOUR

Exemplary Public Alternative School Programs

This chapter includes detailed descriptions of six public alternative schools and programs visited by the author during the 1987–88 and 1988–89 school years. The schools were chosen because they serve a variety of students in terms of age, ability and needs. Two of the schools serve students who have not had a great deal of academic success and have personal needs that conventional schools cannot meet. Two other schools serve students who range from below to above average in academic ability. Lastly, two programs are included that serve primarily above-average students who want an accelerated educational experience.

Each of the six schools and programs described in this chapter represents a different option. They are a learning center, continuation school, open school, school without walls, school within a school program, and magnet elementary program. The schools and programs all have national or regional reputations and have been in existence for a minimum of ten years (the newest option is fifteen years old and the oldest is twenty-one). In addition, five of the six options have conducted evaluations on their effectiveness. While each of the six schools is unique in the option it offers, all have been effective in providing a meaningful educational experience for their students.

VOCATIONAL VILLAGE (LEARNING CENTER)

Located on the industrial southeast side of Portland, Oregon, Vocational Village is housed in a former factory that once made winches for four-wheel-drive vehicles. The school district leased the building in 1972 and transformed it into an alternative vocational school. From the outside the building still looks like a factory, but inside is found a learning center with special resources and programs all under one roof.

Vocational shops are interspersed among classrooms. A large

cafeteria/meeting room is at the center of the complex. There is a delicatessen with a café-like seating area adjacent to it. Students can be found working in small groups or alone. During the fifteen-minute morning break students make their way downstairs to the "Subway" for a game of ping-pong or pool. The building is clean. There is no graffiti or trash. Movement between classes is quiet and orderly. The atmosphere is less that of a school and more of a village at work.

Vocational Village offers a self-paced program that concentrates on basic skills acquisition and vocational training. Students ages 16–21 who have been unsuccessful in conventional high schools may qualify for the program. The typical student at Vocational Village is male, lower income, and employed part or full time. Twenty-two percent of the students are members of minority groups, although an extra effort must be made to attract black students because of the school's location in a predominantly white section of the city.

Vocational Village enrolls approximately 200 day and 60 night students. New students must undergo an entrance interview, diagnostic testing, and a folder check. The interview serves to establish the student's vocational interests and seriousness of purpose. Testing allows assessment of basic skills and identification of any needed remediation. The folder check informs the school about any drug referrals, fines, or other violations that the student might have accumulated at his or her previous high school. Although only 1 percent of applicants are turned down, others "deselect" themselves during the waiting period prior to admission.

New students are enrolled on Tuesdays throughout the school year. During the first day they undergo an orientation meeting with the principal. At this time they learn about the various options offered in the program and have an opportunity to get to know the principal (and vice versa) on an informal level. New students are also introduced to the core values of Vocational Village:

Don't interfere with anyone's education, including your own.
Treat everyone in the building with respect and courtesy.
Respect property: yours, the school's, and other people's.

Students choose one of eight vocational areas in which to concentrate. The eight areas encompass: automotive, graphic arts, food service, metalwork, marketing, childcare, health, and office occupations. Advisory groups consisting of one academic and one vocational teacher and all the students in that vocational group meet at the beginning and end of each school day. This gives the student access to a friendship group of peers and a "home base" from which to operate daily. The two teachers take a special interest in the students in their advisory and serve as counselors for personal as well as school-related matters. Having both vocational and academic teachers in each advisory benefits teachers as well as students, because it creates an interdisciplinary relationship that forces each teacher to see beyond his or her course offerings to the curriculum of the total program.

Twenty-four teachers in eight vocational and nine academic areas offer a seven-period day and a five-period night program. Classes are small, usually including fewer than twenty students, and individualized. Students work at their own pace. The curriculum is performance-based. Students work toward mastery. Teachers establish the necessary criteria for each student, who receives credit rather than a grade on satisfactory completion. One advantage of this approach is that motivated students are able to earn credits faster than they could at a conventional high school.

Students who score below the sixth-grade level in reading during the pre-entry diagnostic testing must enroll in a remedial reading course consisting of prescriptive testing, a low student-teacher ratio, intensive individualized instruction, and large amounts of positive reinforcement. Results have been dramatic. Students average a 1.7 year gain per thirty-five class periods.

Vocational Village offers the entire course of study for high school graduation. The school year is divided into six-week terms. Rather than lose credits for incomplete work, students carry over work into the next term. Attendance is required, although seat time is not linked to earning credit. Prior to graduation students must pass a competency examination required of all students in the Portland school district. Upon successful completion of the exam and accumulation of the necessary credits, students receive a Portland public schools diploma from Vocational Village.

In addition to the regular curriculum, students have the opportunity to take courses at the local community college. Tuition, however, is the responsibility of the student. Credit for community service is another option. Students have served on school district and community committees and attended workshops. Supervision is usually done by the principal, a former social studies teacher who believes strongly in community involvement.

The school also operates a preschool three mornings a week for children in the neighborhood. A modest fee is charged. Students majoring in childcare work in the preschool and earn credit for their efforts. Marketing students operate a delicatessen that provides light snacks during the morning break. Lunch is provided daily by the students who are concentrating in the food service option. This option is the only one of its kind in the Portland school district.

Vocational Village features a strong program of drug counseling. Many of the students have been involved with substance abuse. A drug counselor is on the staff of the school. She conducts daily support group meetings and coursework for elective credit. Her efforts, along with those of the general counselor and the teacher advisory teams, make counseling a strong component of the school. Many of the students have home lives that are less than satisfactory. Personal attention and counseling are essential to their academic and vocational success.

The shops and laboratories of Vocational Village are modern and of excellent quality. For example, the graphic arts component features desktop publishing and computerized typesetting as well as spaces for film processing, binding, and paste-up and layout. Brand new cars and trucks damaged in transit can be found in the automotive shop. The office occupations classroom boasts the latest models of computers used in offices.

Even with these resources and services, the cost of educating a student at Vocational Village is approximately one-half of what it costs Portland at any of its conventional high schools. This is because Vocational Village receives supplemental income from county and state grants for the clientele it serves.

Is Vocational Village having any success with its clientele? The answer appears to be yes. Students have cut their absentee rate in half over what it was when they were enrolled at conventional schools. Each June approximately sixty students receive diplomas and high school equivalency certificates—remarkable, considering that all had been previously unsuccessful in high school.

If school attitude and behavior are evidence, then Vocational Village is having a positive impact on the students it serves. Students are polite and well behaved. There is a sense of pride in the school, reflected in its cleanliness and relaxed orderliness. The school's graduates can be found assisting in classes and serving as role models for students.

The Portland school district must think Vocational Village is an effective option for its students. Vocational Village, along with other options, has become an integral part of the school district. In 1984 the district established a centralized office for alternative education that today oversees some twenty-five programs at the elementary and secondary levels.

OFF-CAMPUS SCHOOL (CONTINUATION SCHOOL)

Bellevue, Washington, is a middle-class suburb of approximately 80,000 people located six miles east of Seattle. Residents of this community are employed primarily in aerospace, computer software production, and international trade. Begun in 1970, Off-Campus School operated out of an old house until 1973, when it moved to its present location, a former church, that was purchased by the Bellevue school district for $100,000. Today the building and grounds are worth several times that amount.

The facilities at Off-Campus are excellent. There is a 25,000-volume library, a comfortably furnished student lounge, ample laboratory and computer equipment, and a new, fully equipped exercise room. A spacious and well supplied daycare center is located in the building. Teachers have their own private offices.

Off-Campus is a continuation school serving students ages 14–21 who have had academic difficulty in conventional schools. Approximately 20 percent have experienced discipline problems. Most have had unsatisfactory attendance. Approximately two-thirds of the students are female.

The causes of the students' problems are varied. Some found work at the conventional schools difficult and were unable to keep up with their peers in the competition for satisfactory grades. For others, the work was easy and the pace too slow. They were bored and resented the lack of intellectual or creative challenge. Still others performed poorly because of chronic physical ailments which kept them from attending school regularly.

Teenage parents are attracted to the school because of its daycare center and teen parent program. A full-time instructional assistant provides care for the children from 9:30 A.M. to 5:30 P.M. four days a week. Parents are expected to spend time in the daycare center and to enroll in a parenting class. A teenage parent support group meets at the school. Approximately 15 percent of Off-Campus's enrollment consists of teenage parents.

Another group represented at the school consists of students in transition from substance abuse and psychological treatment centers. This group comprises about 20 percent of the student body. Off-Campus provides substance abuse support groups and counseling.

In addition to students with school-related problems and family and personal needs, individuals with full-time athletic and artistic commitments—professional ice skaters, musicians, or ballet dancers, for example—are attracted to the school's individualized program of study and flexible hours.

Finally, students who simply want an alternative educational experience are attracted to the school. They may be looking for a more personal, one-to-one relationship with their teachers, a relationship that is very difficult to obtain in a conventional public school. They may also want the opportunity to pursue work independently and the flexibility to progress at their own rate.

Off-Campus has an enrollment of some 200 to 225 students and a faculty of eleven teachers and one head teacher. The head teacher combines administrative with teaching responsibilities. The teachers are expected to be counselors as well as subject matter specialists. Each is assigned fifteen to twenty students to advise and monitor closely during their time at the school.

With the exception of family living, cooking, some physical education classes, and a writing group, all subjects are taken by students on an individual basis. Students work on contracts they have negotiated with their teachers. Credits are earned by completing a certain number of hours (typically seventy-five to eighty). A student's level of performance must be at "A" or "B" level, as determined by the teacher. Students must also satisfy district-mandated student learning objectives (SLOs), which are incorporated into their contracted work. Students work toward a diploma from Off-Campus School; there is no high school GED program. The school does not serve special education students.

Students enroll for two credits at a time. They must make two or three appointments per week with their teacher for each credit. The appointment time is used to have work checked by teachers and to receive new assignments. Visitors to the school will not see groups of students engaged in whole-class instruction with their teacher; instead, they will observe students working one-on-one with a teacher, with other students, or simply by themselves.

Off-Campus operates year round and does not divide the school year into quarters or semesters. Students work continuously to complete credits. Upon completion of a credit a new contract is begun. Less able or motivated students may take more time to complete contract requirements than more able or motivated ones. This flexibility allows students to pursue graduation at their own rate. Graduation from Off-Campus may occur at any time during the year.

A variety of texts and materials are available for student and teacher use. Primary sources are the most frequently used materials, especially in English and social studies. Teachers attempt to incorporate materials that are at the ability level of each student they are working with, individualizing curriculum as well as instruction.

While most credits earned are from completing work from text books and course-related materials provided by teachers, opportunities exist for students to pursue independent, off-campus work of their own. One student spent the summer on the Olympic peninsula working with a University of Washington professor studying glaciers. The professor wrote an evaluation of the student's work, which the student submitted along with a required report to his teacher for one credit in science. Another spent six weeks at the University of Oregon School of Oceanography at Newport. She reported back to her teacher at two-week intervals to turn in assignments and receive feedback on previous assignments. She too earned a credit in science. A third traveled to the southwestern United States to study Native American architecture. She kept a journal and turned in related papers for a social studies credit. Still another student traveled to the Soviet Union and as part of a requirement for his English course wrote an article about his travels for the *Christian Science Monitor*. In each case, travel and related expenses were the responsibility of the student.

Students may also receive community service credits by volunteering for a variety of service activities in the community. Working as a candy striper at a local hospital, assisting in a nursing home, helping at a recycling center, and volunteering in a drug treatment center are examples of such activities. In addition, periodically scheduled fieldtrips and special activities to museums, exhibits, concerts, and plays complement and enrich coursework.

Students may dual enroll at any of the district's conventional high schools to take courses not offered at Off-Campus. Students may also take courses at the local community college and receive high school and college credit simultaneously. The student, however, must pay the tuition. One student, at her own expense, enrolled as a freshman at Western Washington University before completing her high school graduating requirements. Off-Campus accepted college coursework completed at Western Washington with a grade of "B" and counted it toward her high school graduation requirements.

Annually, Off-Campus sends 60 percent of its students to postsecondary education. That is comparable to the four conventional high schools in Bellevue. While Off-Campus graduates are more likely to enroll in two-year and vocational colleges than their peers, a number have been accepted to such prestigious colleges and universities as Harvard, the University of Chicago, Berkeley, and Princeton.

Because of its varied student body, Off-Campus avoids being "typed" as a school for "druggies" or "losers" or "weirdos." Some public alternative schools and programs are subject to negative stereotyping within their communities because of the student clientele they serve. Off-Campus School is able to avoid such narrow categorization because of the variety of its student body and the success of its comprehensive and highly individualistic academic program.

The success of the program is confirmed by the school's full accreditation by the Northwest Association of Schools and Colleges and an evaluation conducted by the University of Washington. A 1988 survey of one third of the state's public schools, including Off-Campus, conducted by the University revealed a positive learning climate among Off-Campus students and teachers significantly higher than at other public schools. The school's waiting list is further testimony to its appeal among high school-age students in Bellevue.

ST. PAUL OPEN SCHOOL (OPEN SCHOOL)

The Open School is located in a former elementary school in a middle-class neighborhood of St. Paul, Minnesota. The school enrolls approximately 350 K–12 students who reflect the ethnic and socioeconomic composition of St. Paul's public schools. A majority of the students are female. Enrollment is evenly divided between the early learning center (grades K–6) and the older learning center (grades 7–12). There are eight teachers in the early learning center (ELC) and nine in the older learning center (OLC).

With the exception of kindergartners, who are taught in a self-contained classroom, students in ELC are placed in cross-age groups and taught by several teachers. Primary groups include students ages 6–9 and intermediate groups include students ages 10–12. Cross-age grouping continues in OLC, with most courses enrolling students from several grade levels.

Cross-age grouping allows both fast and slow students to proceed at their own rates more easily and with less comparison to the progress of others. In a primary group, a 9-year-old may be doing first-grade level work while a 6-year-old is doing third grade work. At OLC a slow 15-year-old may enroll in a science class designed primarily for seventh- through ninth-graders. Likewise, an advanced 13-year-old may enroll in a math class for tenth- through twelfth-graders. In a K–12 school, cross-age grouping makes it possible for highly motivated and able elementary students to enroll in selected secondary courses. For students who need more concentrated remediation, a special education resource room is located in the school.

Open School's K–12 configuration has a number of advantages over a strictly elementary or secondary school. One benefit of having primary- and secondary-age children in the same building is the softening effect the younger children have on the older ones. It is difficult for a 15-year-old to be a "tough" guy or keep a "hard" pose when a 7-year-old asks him for help. It is not uncommon to see frequent displays of affection in the hallways between older students and their adopted mascots.

Older students serve as role models for younger ones and help raise the level of maturity within the school. It is not uncommon to see OLC students in ELC classrooms assisting the teacher, tutoring students, or cleaning up the room. Helping out is particularly rewarding to slower OLC students, who can make a contribution to younger ones and in the process enhance their own sense of self-worth.

Parents and students are attracted to the school for a variety of reasons. Some are dissatisfied with their neighborhood school and want a change. For some, Open School is seen as a step up to a better school and a safer neighborhood. Others want a more personal atmosphere and a smaller school. Some students have difficulty fitting in at larger schools, particularly comprehensive high schools, and fall between the cracks. Open School gives them the personal attention they need. Some students have unusual schedules that make attendance at conventional schools difficult. Individuals studying to be professional musicians or athletes, as well as those with full-time jobs, are unable to keep a 9:00 A.M. to 3:00 P.M. schedule. Still others are attracted to the flexible curriculum and emphasis upon personal freedom and responsibility.

As its name implies, Open School offers a less structured and less teacher-directed education than a conventional school. Classrooms are more informal. Movement and student talk are accepted. Students address teachers by their first names. In ELC, primary and intermediate students are scheduled for a daily two-and-one-half-hour morning block of math and reading. After lunch and a thirty-minute advisory period, students attend three forty-five-minute choice classes which they have chosen with their parents' permission. Choices include bookmaking, collectors' club, logo class, creative drama, Spanish, puppet theater, puffin math, recorder, woodshop, and sewing, among others.

Both ELC and OLC have fifteen-minute advisory periods at the beginning and end of each day. Advisory consists of a small group of students assigned to a teacher who takes a personal interest in the academic and interpersonal progress of his or her advisees for a period of several years. Advisory time is devoted to discussing individual goals, conducting school business, and establishing peer friendships.

There are no grades or course requirements at the Open School. Students receive written evaluations instead of grades from their teachers each quarter if they are in ELC and each semester if they are in OLC. Teachers also receive written evaluations from their students at these times. Open School students are exempted from state graduation requirements. Students do not earn credits toward graduation but rather demonstrate competencies in the following six areas:

- Career education, including post-high school plans, job-seeking skills, and career investigation
- Community involvement and current issues, including learning from the community, service to the community, service to the school, and current issues
- Consumer awareness, including personal finance and mastery of a math competency test
- Cultural awareness, including focus on one's own culture and two other cultures
- Personal and interpersonal skills, including emphasis on a healthy body, group process, and coherent communication
- Information finding, including use of reference and research materials, data collection, and interviewing techniques.

Students must have their work in the six areas approved, or "validated," by teachers and appropriate adults. A total of seventeen validations is required for graduation. Students must compile a graduation portfolio with documentation of the seventeen validations from the six required areas. While most of the validations are accomplished through successful completion of school coursework, many are done outside school by demonstrating competency to a qualified adult.

Portfolios include letters and other documentation indicating successful completion of each of the required seventeen validations. A professor of music, furniture store owner, or restaurateur may indicate competency in career education. Participating in a church choir, volunteering in a nursing home, serving as a teacher's aide, or helping in an election campaign might be used to satisfy requirements in community involvement and current issues. A banker, business manager, or insurance agent could attest to consumer awareness. A Greek Orthodox priest, multicultural resource teacher, or head of the Asian/Pacific Learning Resource Center may validate cultural awareness. Documentation from a nurse, athletic coach, YMCA director, or editor could satisfy the personal and interpersonal skills requirement. A librarian, English teacher, or computer specialist might document ability in information finding. Upon acceptance of the portfolio by the student's committee, he or she qualifies for a city-wide diploma granted by the St. Paul school district.

Great emphasis is placed on community involvement and experience. On any given day 10 percent of the student body is away from school, involved in some kind of community experience. A three-week interim period between semesters at OLC and between second and third quarter at ELC allows students to pursue all-day (OLC) and half-day (ELC) independent and structured projects involving the community. During interim travel out of state, all-day local fieldtrips, community projects, and special intensive activities are undertaken.

Open School's competency-based curriculum insures accountability while allowing flexibility for student determination of how the competency requirements will be met and at what rate they will be accomplished. Motivated and able students may complete their graduation requirements early. In the past a number of students graduated early and left for college and other interests. Today, fewer students are leaving early because of recent changes in public education legislation in Minnesota, which have made remaining in school much more attractive.

Minnesota now permits public high school students to take courses in other school districts and at public and private colleges and universities within the state free of charge if those courses or subjects are not offered in the students' local school district. As a result of this legislation, students at the Open School and at other public schools in Minnesota are enrolling in colleges and universities and taking coursework that may be applied to their freshman year when they do apply to college. Within a four-mile radius of the Open School one can find the colleges of Macalester, St. Thomas, Hamline, Concordia, and St. Catherine, as well as the University of Minnesota. Students who do not wish to take college and university courses may enroll part time in other public schools in St. Paul to take courses not available at the Open School. For example, a student who wants to pursue advanced mathematics, foreign language, music, or automotive shop will take those subjects at a neighborhood school because they are not offered at the Open School.

Students who are motivated and have personal goals clearly in view benefit most from the emphasis on personal freedom and responsibility at the Open School. However, unmotivated or immature students can experience difficulty. In 1988, twelve of the school's thirty-six seniors failed to graduate because they did not complete their validations successfully. Some of them thought that passing competencies would be easy, so easy that they did not feel the need to take their classes and community experiences seriously. As a result, they spent extra time at the school in order to graduate.

When compared to other public school students in St. Paul, Open School students perform quite well. Norm-referenced standardized tests administered yearly by the school district show Open School students to be at district levels in language arts, significantly above them in reading, and slightly below them in math. Approximately 60 percent of Open School students go on to postsecondary education, a slightly higher rate than that of the district as a whole.

Ironically, Open School's success has contributed to a slight decrease in the numbers and the ability level of incoming students over the past few years. In 1971, when the Open School was started, it was one of only a handful of public alternatives in St. Paul. Since that time, public alternative schools and programs in the St. Paul school district have grown dramatically. Today, the district offers fourteen elementary and seventeen secondary alternative schools and programs. They include such options as creative arts, science, Montessori, Chinese, mathematics, gifted and talented, international studies, and communications, as well as a new high-tech alternative school called the Saturn School of Tomorrow. Open School must now compete for students who have many options to choose from. In addition, some of the early enthusiasm for open education has waned in recent years; today's parents and students are more conservative, less willing to take risks. Still, Open School provides an excellent program and opportunity for those individuals who seek an education that encourages freedom and responsibility.

LEARNING UNLIMITED (SCHOOL WITHIN A SCHOOL)

Located in Indianapolis, North Central High School is the largest four-year high school in Indiana, with an enrollment of some 3,200 students. The high school is an enormous complex with up-to-date facilities. It has its own indoor swimming pool, planetarium, and private security patrol. It also houses one of the country's best-known alternative programs, Learning Unlimited.

Learning Unlimited (LU) is a school within a school that serves some 250 North Central students. Students are selected for LU after they submit an application and undergo an interview. The primary criterion for selection is an expressed seriousness to participate in the program. All students enroll on a part-time basis—some for only one period, others for up to six periods. The average is three periods out of a seven-period day.

Like students, most LU faculty spend part of their time in the program and part in the regular high school. Out of eight LU teachers, five have split assignments. A head teacher directs the program, combining administrative with teaching responsibilities. There are disadvantages to using part-time faculty in an alternative program. Loyalties are often divided between the alternative and regular school. Coordination of meetings and related activities can be difficult. Adjustment to the differing classroom behaviors and expectations of alternative and conventional students is not always easy.

Yet there are also advantages in such an arrangement. It is easier to build rapport and gain program credibility when alternative teachers can be seen working successfully in conventional settings. Split teaching assignments allow the introduction of alternative ideas into the conventional curriculum. For example, using the community as a resource is the major ingredient of LU. That practice has crept into conventional courses as a result of alternative teachers' introducing it into the regular curriculum.

The part-time participation of students in LU is not a problem. The program is not designed to be an all-inclusive alternative to the conventional high school. Rather, it is an elective program for students who want an experiential component in their educational program. LU makes no attempt to offer the full high school curriculum. Students needing foreign languages, mathematics, or science must take those courses in the conventional high school. LU offers coursework in the social sciences, English, photography, film study, art, and physical education. Its primary focus and reason for being, however, is community experience and volunteer service.

Begun in 1974, LU took its inspiration from the Walkabout model of Maurice Gibbons of Simon Fraser University in British Columbia. Gibbons proposed an educational experience modeled somewhat after the Australian aborigine practice of Walkabout. The idea was to provide students with community-related experiences that would prepare them for the transition from youth to adulthood and encourage the notion of lifelong learning. While the ambitiousness and length of community experience has diminished somewhat since the program's inception, the main purpose remains.

Students are attracted to LU for a variety of reasons. Many realize the usefulness of having community experiences on their resumes when they apply for competitive colleges and universities. Some are dissatisfied with the inflexibility of conventional schooling and want a more relevant educational experience. Others are seeking a closer personal relationship with their teachers. Still others want the opportunity to work independently on projects of their choice, and a few just want to get out of school during the day. Some high-risk students are referred to LU by their counselors, in hopes that program will help turn them around. On the whole, LU students are more motivated, assertive, independent, and socially aware than their conventional North Central counterparts. Interestingly, the majority of LU students have traditionally been female.

Upon entering the program, a student agrees to undertake a minimum of twenty-four hours of community service each eighteen-week semester. Most students put in considerably more time than the minimum. Ninth- and tenth-graders participate in group experiences, such as fieldtrips to museums, social agencies, retirement homes, and so forth. They are transported in one of two school-owned vans by LU's community coordinator.

Eleventh- and twelfth-graders sign up for individual community projects and provide their own transportation. A list of community projects is provided by the coordinator, and students choose from it or find projects on their own. Sample projects from the list include serving as teacher's aides, office assistants, tour guides, camp counselors, and assistants to artists, photographers, and musicians. Three community projects undertaken in 1988 that illustrate the types of activities and responsibilities LU students assume are peer jury duty, teacher's aide at the Indiana School for the Deaf, and visitor at a retirement center.

Peer jury operates out of the Marion County prosecutor's office. First-time juvenile offenders pleading guilty to a misdemeanor have the option of being sentenced by a judge or by a jury of their peers. Students from LU and other Indianapolis area schools meet weekly with defendants, read the police reports, and decide on appropriate sentences. At the Indiana School for the Deaf, two students volunteer one morning each week in an elementary classroom as teacher's aides. They help the teacher prepare classroom materials, work one-on-one with students on teacher-directed assignments, and assist on occasional class fieldtrips. In a major undertaking, thirty LU students were paired with thirty retirees having career experience in areas of particular interest to their youthful visitors. The project, called Living Documents, was designed to make history come alive for students and to give senior citizens a more accurate picture of today's youth. The project was undertaken in cooperation with a nursing home and a local church. Students visited the retirees weekly, sharing experiences and interests.

Many of the community projects are related to coursework taken at LU. Students in photography and art classes may choose to work with a community resource person in one of those fields. Projects such as assisting in election campaigns and government offices tie naturally into social studies. Students enrolled in English classes may volunteer as teacher's aides or assist at radio and television stations. Work in community projects is important, counting for 20 percent of a student's semester course grade.

Students must keep a journal and timecard of their activities. The timecard is signed by the community resource person and returned to the student's LU teacher at the end of each six-week grading period. The resource person must also submit to LU an evaluation of the student's performance. The journal, timecard, and resource person's evaluation become the basis for the student's community project grade. Students receive letter grades at LU.

Classes at LU are scheduled to allow students time for their community experiences. Typically they meet four times a week, leaving one day free for community work. Extensive use of contracts is made to allow students to do school work on their own time. Teachers and students agree on mutually acceptable standards of performance and negotiate a final grade on completion of the contract. Independent study is another option for students who wish to pursue a subject of interest in greater depth. LU teachers believe in providing choices and freedom to students and expect responsibility in return. Internships, which are longer-term and more ambitious community projects, are no longer offered because of increased graduation requirements and longer school hours.

LU is governed through town meetings held biweekly. Program business and policy matters are discussed and voted on by students and teachers. Discipline problems are handled by a student review board made up of two seniors, two juniors, one sophomore, and one freshman. The board determines and administers punishments.

Students who take advantage of the opportunities provided by LU experience personal growth and develop a sense of satisfaction from making decisions and helping others. Follow-up surveys of former students and their parents reveal that the program has had a great deal of success in these areas. Responses to an independent external study of LU conducted in 1986 found that 92 percent of graduates and 85 percent of parents rated LU more effective in preparing students for the future than any other part of their high school experience. Ninety-six percent of graduates and 78 percent of parents rated LU more effective in developing personal skills than any other part of their high school experience.

LU has demonstrated success not only in personal and affective goals but in academic performance as well. Results of the 1986 study found the average combined SAT scores of LU students to be sixty-nine points above the average for North Central students, and eighty-four points above the national average. Ninety percent of LU students enroll in postsecondary institutions. Many are accepted to such competitive institutions as Northwestern, the University of Chicago, Earlham, and Brandeis. Survey results indicated that 66 percent of graduates and 78 percent of parents rated LU more effective in developing academic skills than any other part of their high school experience.

Perhaps the best measure of LU's success can be found in the comments of its students: "I got to meet a lot of new people and become closer to others because of the close family atmosphere"; "I can honestly say I learned how to learn; I felt comfortable and uninhibited because of the freedom LU gave me"; "Independence, responsibility, and leadership." These comments reflect the sense of community and belonging students experience at LU. While the opportunity of an independent and academically challenging experience draws many students to the program, it is the closeness and personal attention they receive from teachers that keeps them at LU.

ENVIRONMENTAL EDUCATION PROGRAM
(MAGNET ELEMENTARY PROGRAM)

Grand Rapids, Michigan, has been a long-time proponent of alternative education. In the early 1970s it gained a national reputation for its innovative programs and cooperative relationship with Indiana University's Alternative School Teacher Education Program. While the number of programs has diminished somewhat and the relationship with Indiana University no longer exists, Grand Rapids continues to attract attention for the alternative programs that remain. Of these, perhaps the best known is the Environmental Education Program (EEP), begun in 1973.

The EEP currently serves some 115–120 students evenly distributed between two sites, the John Ball Zoo and the Blandford Nature Center. It is designed for academically capable sixth-graders who are performing at or above grade level in math and reading and who are self-motivated, self-disciplined, and able to work independently. Students are selected in the spring of their fifth-grade year by teacher nomination and principal endorsement. Parents may nominate their children, but such nominations are subject to principal endorsement.

The forty-two elementary schools in Grand Rapids have been divided into two geographic regions, one of which feeds students to a school at the John Ball Zoo site and the other to a school at the Blandford Nature Center site. Each elementary school is given a certain number of slots to fill. This insures that the EEP draws a student body representative of the school district's ethnic and social-class composition. Approximately 71 percent of the students are white and 29 percent are minority. In addition, a number of places are reserved for parochial school students who choose to spend their sixth-grade year in the program. This latter practice is a concession to the large and influential private school population in Grand Rapids. Children are bused from their elementary school to the Zoo and the Nature Center at district expense.

The EEP is staffed by four teachers, two at each site, and administered by an elementary principal who divides his responsibilities between the program and a regular K–6 school. The split assignment means competition for the principal's attention and time. While not an ideal arrangement, the program manages to operate effectively because of the experience and expertise of its teachers. Teacher experience in the EEP ranges from a low of nine to a high of seventeen years.

Considerable autonomy is given to the teachers for program development and implementation. Each school operates independently of the other, with slightly different curricular and instructional emphases. These differences, as well as similarities, will become apparent as activities at the two schools are described.

Blandford School

The Blandford School, located in a former elementary school that also houses a preschool and readiness kindergarten program, occupies two regular classrooms and a computer lab. The lab contains 20 Apple II GS computers, awarded through a grant by the Apple Computer Corporation. Two teachers, one elementary and one secondary science, and a teacher's aide comprise the staff. The School is adjacent to the Blandford Nature Center, a 140-acre county environmental education center, with nature trails, a thirty-acre working farm, a small live animal collection, and a visitor interpretation center. Nature School students use the Center as an outdoor classroom year round. Teachers and students divide their time evenly between outdoor and in-school instruction.

Outdoor activities follow the seasons. During late summer and early autumn students are introduced to the flora and fauna of the Nature Center. They serve as trail guides to the many primary school groups that come to the Center on fieldtrips. A three-day campout introduces the students to outdoor skills. During the winter outdoor activities include cross country skiing, snowshoeing, bird watching, and snow study. This is also the time of special projects and preparation for the spring. Early spring brings warmer weather and maple syrup. Students tap maple trees, collect and boil sap in the Center's sugaring shed, make maple syrup, and resume their trail guide responsibilities. Teachers and students undertake a one-week survival campout just prior to the end of the school year. Students are expected to put into practice the outdoor skills they have learned during the year.

In addition to these outdoor activities, students operate a commercial egg business year round on the Nature Center's farm. Students buy 100 laying hens, feed and care for them, and market the eggs. They even built the coop where the chickens are kept. This ongoing business combines a number of academic skills, most notably math and science.

The curriculum is interdisciplinary. Subjects are not taught in isolation from one another but rather combined under themes or projects like the egg business. Teacher-made materials predominate. Themes like "pioneer living" allow the integration of a variety of disciplines. Students study Indians and settlers for social studies, read *The Yearling* or *Westwind Woods* for literature, learn pioneer songs and games for music and physical education, and make natural dyes and wild tea for science. Much of the learning is hands-on and student-directed. A cooperative learning model or team approach is encouraged by teachers and practiced by students.

Students are split into two equal groups. In the morning one group has the elementary-trained teacher for language arts and social studies, while the other group has the secondary-trained teacher for math and science. In the afternoon the groups switch teachers. The two teachers coordinate much of their instruction and work cooperatively together. Homework is given four nights a week, and student work is graded. Narrative progress reports supplement letter grades, which are given three times a year.

Students make considerable use of the computer lab to carry out experiments and record results. The computer facilitates data analyses and the writing of reports. Keyboarding, database, spreadsheet, and word processing are the computer skills taught to students. The teachers oversee the computer lab and the teacher's aide assists students.

In addition to the egg business, other major projects, such as the annual science and international fairs, are undertaken. Most of the work is done at school to insure that students, not parents, are the primary contributors to the projects. Extensive use is made of community resource persons, such as astronomers, bird experts, Native American craftsmen, and parents with particular skills and interests. Always the focus is on nature and the environment.

John Ball Zoo School

The John Ball Zoo School is located on the grounds of the John Ball Zoo. Operated by the city of Grand Rapids, the zoo contains some 500 animals on thirty acres, with an additional 100 acres of fields, woods, and creeks. The school makes use of two classrooms, a small lab, and a large seminar/library room on the ground floor of the zoo's two-story education building. Two teachers, one elementary and one secondary science, provide instruction, assisted by a teacher's aide. Students have both teachers, each for an entire day, every other day. The elementary teacher is responsible for English and social studies, the secondary teacher for math and science.

The theme of nature continues in the curriculum of the Zoo School, but the emphasis moves from plants to animals. Students spend 25 percent of their time working and studying outside of the classroom in the zoo. Every student adopts an animal, learns about it, and visits it weekly. On Tuesdays and Thursdays a professional zoologist employed by the zoo instructs students on various aspects of animal life. Zoo keepers also give occasional presentations. Every other Friday students spend two hours working in the zoo raking, gardening, fertilizing, and landscaping. During the year students work toward the privilege of becoming junior zoo keepers. In the spring approximately 20 percent of them are chosen to spend half days for a six-week period assisting adult zoo keepers. In the past a greater percentage of students were chosen to become junior zoo keepers and a greater amount of time was allowed for them to work in the zoo. Increased insurance costs and concern over liability have reduced the time and level of participation.

As at Blandford, the Zoo School curriculum is interdisciplinary. Teachers develop their own materials rather than use those of publishers. Projects are the main instructional approach and allow for the combination of a variety of academic subjects and skills under topics or themes. For example, as students study their adopted animal they also learn about the geography of its natural habitat and environmental issues related to its survival. Artwork and creative writing are drawn from knowledge gained about the animal's existence.

Students are expected to undertake individual and group projects and are taught the necessary research and study skills to be successful independent learners. To this end, the academic year is divided into three semesters, each with a specific focus. In the fall students work intensively on developing basic skills, such as notetaking, outlining, speech communication, and basic concepts in zoology and botany, as well as language arts and math.

During the winter students undertake group projects on such topics as the Amazon, astronomy, Michigan habitats, and so forth. Students learn to work together and individually to complete a variety of tasks related to the overall topic. Each student researches an aspect of the topic that contributes to the overall group project. For example, a project on the Amazon will have students working independently on such areas as the geography, indigenous culture, animals, and natural resources of the region. Upon completion of their individual topics, the students present the entire project as a group effort.

By spring students should be ready to undertake major, in-depth, individual projects on more specialized topics, for example, solar energy, behavior modification of rats, electromagnets, incubation of eggs, and animal habitats. During a six-week period, half days are set aside for students to work on their projects. To insure success, parents and students sign a contract indicating commitment and a willingness to provide the necessary materials for completion of the project. Students must also keep a daily diary of their progress for teacher inspection.

For those students who are not ready to work independently, structured projects are assigned by the teachers. These projects consist of prescribed tasks and a completion schedule for students to follow. Teachers closely monitor student progress along the way. Performance updates are periodically completed for each student in order to keep parents informed. In addition, students receive report cards every six weeks. Letter grades are given in five areas: academic, classroom responsibility, independent study skills, problem solving, and attitude.

The goal of the Environmental Education Program is the development of life-long learners, individuals who will have the skill, experience, and desire to learn on their own in the future. It is an ambitious goal, one that is not achieved by every student. Each year one or two students find themselves misplaced and return to their regular elementary school. A few students who remain in the program find it difficult to become independent learners and struggle to succeed. For the vast majority, however, the EEP is a success.

A 1987 evaluation conducted by the Grand Rapids school district revealed that parents and students had very positive feelings about the EEP. Ninety-eight percent of parents surveyed described the program as beneficial or very beneficial, and 86 percent indicated the program was very useful in their children's other classes. Eighty-eight percent of students responded that the EEP classes will be helpful to them in later life, and 82 percent indicated that the things learned in school were useful in the real world.

Assessment of the academic achievement of EEP graduates found that the program had a long-term positive effect on students' reading and math scores. Former EEP graduates were tested in their junior and senior high school years and the results indicated that the high level of academic achievement demonstrated in elementary school was sustained throughout the students' educational experience. Furthermore, parents reported that the EEP was very helpful in developing such nonacademic characteristics as self-confidence, the acceptance of responsibility, and the undertaking of challenges among their children. The success of the EEP depends not only on the commitment of the Grand Rapids school district but on the cooperation and support of the city, which operates the John Ball Zoo, and the county, which operates the Blandford Nature Center. For the past seventeen years the three have worked together effectively to provide an outstanding alternative educational experience for the children of Grand Rapids.

PHILADELPHIA PARKWAY (SCHOOL WITHOUT WALLS)

Philadelphia's Parkway program is among the oldest and best known public alternative schools in the country. Begun in 1969 as a school without walls, Parkway gained a national reputation for its extensive use of city resources, particularly those along the Benjamin Franklin Parkway between the Philadelphia Art Museum and downtown. Classes were held in banks, hospitals, museums, and various social agencies. Community resource people frequently served as instructors in these classes.

Parkway continues to be a school without walls, but it is a bit more circumscribed now than it was in its earlier years. The initial enthusiasm for and extensive use of the community has diminished somewhat. A more conservative educational climate prevails today, characterized by increased state-mandated credit requirements, introduction of a citywide standardized curriculum, and a more pragmatic student body. Fewer elective credits are available to students, a more prescribed course of study has reduced curricular flexibility, and fewer students are willing to take educational risks. The result is that, while virtually all students in the late 1960s and early 1970s participated in community-based coursework and related activities, only 25 percent of the students did so in the 1980s. In an effort to increase student participation, Parkway students in 1988–89 were required to earn at least one credit (120 hours) in a variety of community learning experiences.

Since its beginning in 1969, Parkway has grown dramatically. Enrollment has gone from 150 students housed in one unit to more than 900 distributed among four units. Parkway is a high school that includes grades 9–12. Students sign up for the program during the second semester of the eighth grade. They may also apply for admission as ninth-, tenth-, or eleventh-graders, depending on the availability of openings. Students are expected to have at least a "C" average in their previous coursework, although some are admitted who may have had less than a "C" average in one or more courses. Behavior and attendance at previous schools are considered even more important in student selection. Parkway is a magnet option within the Philadelphia school district and must reflect the ethnic and social-class composition of the school district. Approximately 75 percent of Parkway's students are minority group members.

Students are placed in one of the four units, which together comprise the Parkway program. Each unit is located in a different part of the city. The four units are: Gamma, City Center, Zeta, and Spring Garden. The school day typically consists of six periods that start at 8:30 A.M. and end at 2:30 P.M., although schedule variations exist at each of the units.

The largest of the Parkway units is Gamma, located on the west side of Philadelphia next to the University of Pennsylvania. Here 260 students and thirteen teachers operate out of an old two-story house that reminds one of structures popular among alternative schools in the 1960s. Gamma takes advantage of university facilities through regularly scheduled courses and special offerings. Tuesdays are set aside as a special day for laboratory work, special interest classes, fieldtrips, and library work, much of it on the University of Pennsylvania campus. Community resource people come to Gamma on Tuesdays to present scheduled classes in such areas as black history, music, health, and physical education.

Science is emphasized at Gamma. Sixty percent of the students enroll in chemistry and 30 percent in physics. Both percentages are considerably above the national average and reflect the success Gamma has had in attracting students with an interest in science. The success is due in large part to the program's excellent reputation. In 1985 the teacher named outstanding science teacher in the Delaware Valley was from Gamma unit.

Center City is located downtown on the ground floor of an office building that formerly housed a business college. There are approximately 250 students and thirteen teachers at this unit. A humanities emphasis, with the downtown as the focus, characterizes the curriculum at City Center. Literature and writing are stressed. Students read novels and plays and then watch them being performed at the Philadelphia Festival and Annenberg Subscription theaters. Students are encouraged to enter citywide writing contests to develop and hone writing skills. Poets and artists in residence share real-life experiences and skills with students to enhance a humanities perspective.

In addition to activities in the humanities, some students make use of city hall and its various government offices. Some participate in a program called Legal Philadelphia. In this program students visit courts, corrections facilities, and attorneys' offices to learn about legal-related activities. Law Enforcement and Preparation (LEAP) is another program students may undertake. LEAP coordinates competitions in organizing and presenting court cases, which train students in debate techniques and critical-thinking skills.

On the north side of Philadelphia is Zeta unit, comprised of 220 students and eleven teachers in a traditional school building adjacent to Temple University. Here are housed Parkway's only art, computer, gifted, and special education programs. Students with these interests or needs enroll at this unit. As in Gamma unit, Zeta students take advantage of university facilities. In addition to their regularly scheduled course offerings at school, students may take university courses free of charge on the Temple campus. Health, physical education, and law-related courses are among the more popular offerings. Instructors are usually graduate students attending the university.

The least urban of the four Parkway units is Spring Garden. In this unit, 200 students and eleven teachers operate out of a three-story building on the campus of Spring Garden College. The college is in an attractive section of historic Germantown and offers a bucolic alternative to the urban locations of the other three units. "A tree-lined oasis" is how one faculty member described Spring Garden.

Germantown is the focus of community experiences for Spring Garden students. Two or three times a month the unit takes half the day off to conduct fieldtrips to various cultural and historical sights. Historical buildings, theater guilds, and the arboretum are among the most popular attractions. Resource people are frequently used to enhance course offerings and community experiences. Professional musicians and artists are regular participants. During the orchestra season students attend rehearsals of the Philadelphia Orchestra. If there is a curricular bias at Spring Garden, it is toward the visual and performing arts.

While each unit has its own identity and curricular emphasis, all participate in the program's community-based electives, which are at the heart of the school without walls concept. Students may enroll in community volunteer activities for elective credit. Placement in these activities is coordinated through the central Parkway office by a community coordinator. A partial list of typical activities includes hospital volunteer, teacher's aide, visitor at a geriatric center, children's tutor, office aide to a congressional or state representative, clerical aide to a veterinarian, and court intern. Students who wish to pursue independent study, perhaps related to their community experience, may do so through their tutorial (advisory) teacher, with whom they meet daily. A contract that establishes criteria acceptable to student and teacher is agreed upon. Students earn grades for all work and receive a Parkway diploma upon successful completion of the program.

The attraction of Parkway is as varied as its student body. Much of the information about the school passes by word of mouth. Most students hear about Parkway from friends or relatives. Some want the opportunity to take college courses. Others seek the challenge and freedom of a community-based educational experience. Many want the close personal relationship between teachers and students that Parkway is known for. Like conventional high schools, Parkway offers a variety of extracurricular activities, such as sports, cheerleading, and clubs that draw students from all four of the units. A number of students select the school for its athletic program. Parkway has been particularly successful in boys basketball and girls volleyball competition within the Philadelphia city league and offers the city's only coed varsity soccer team. More than a few Parkway athletes have received college scholarships as a result of their efforts. A number of parents have selected the school because it represents a better school in a safer neighborhood for their children.

As one of the school district's magnet options, Parkway must compete with other schools for students. Philadelphia has among its options the High Schools of Performing Arts, Engineering and Science, and International Affairs. In addition, Central High and Girls High remain as the city's selective academic options. Students who are unable to get their first choice sometimes select Parkway as their second choice.

This is not to say Parkway is an easy school to enroll in or graduate from. The attrition rate runs at about 30 percent a year. Some students fail to take advantage of the freedom offered and responsibility expected by teachers. Students who need considerable structure and direction experience difficulty. As with all alternative schools, Parkway is not for everyone. However, those who complete the program do well. Approximately 70 percent of Parkway graduates go on to postsecondary education. For students who are motivated to learn and who are self-directed, Parkway provides a unique and rewarding educational option. Outstanding universities, community experiences rich in variety, an attentive faculty, and the flexibility to pursue personal goals make Parkway still one of the most innovative and interesting options in public alternative education today.

CONCLUSIONS

The six schools and programs described in this chapter represent a variety of options for students of different ages, abilities, and needs. While each option is unique, all share the characteristics of public alternative schools and programs outlined in Chapter 3: smallness, concern for the whole student, supportive environment, and sense of community/clear mission. In addition, the long term success of these options demonstrates an ability to respond to changing educational climates within their respective communities.

Meeting the Effectiveness Criteria

Smallness. The six schools and programs are relatively small in size and operate with a limited number of staff and students. The smallest, the Environmental Education Program, enrolls some 115 students, while Parkway, the largest, enrolls more than 900. Enrollment at each of the other four options is between 200 and 250.

Parkway, with an enrollment of 900, may not appear to qualify as a small school. Yet it maintains smallness by dividing the program into four self-contained units or sites of 200–250 students each. Open School, with 350 students at one location, also appears to be too large for an effective alternative school; but 350 students is not large for a K–12 school. Open School further divides its students into learning centers of 175 students each.

Smallness opens up opportunities for greater student participation in school-related activities, which is one of the attractions for Parkway students. Smallness also facilitates a family atmosphere and closer personal relationships between students and teachers, a feature noted by Learning Unlimited students. Smallness contributes to the informality at Off-Campus, Open School, and Learning Unlimited, where students address teachers by their first names. Finally, smallness allows students to pursue independent learning experiences and out-of-school activities that would be difficult in schools and programs of conventional size.

Concern for the whole student. For the most part, these schools and programs serve an identified clientele (students with academic difficulty, teenage parents, full-time athletes and artists, highly capable sixth-graders, etc.). Serving a particular clientele allows the schools and programs to focus on the special needs of their students. Unlike conventional schools, which must be all things to all students, these alternative schools can concentrate their resources and efforts on aspects of particular need to their student clientele and thus provide a more effective program.

Flexible school hours, daycare, and a teen parent program at Off-Campus; counseling, support groups, and vocational shops at Vocational Village; supervised community placement at Learning Unlimited and Parkway; early graduation at Open School; and a zoo and nature center at the Environmental Education Program—all these have been designed to meet a variety of affective as well as cognitive needs among the particular student clientele served. Because these schools and programs serve a limited population of students, their options can provide a complete educational program for the whole student.

Supportive environment. An atmosphere of mutual respect among students and teachers exists at all of these schools and programs because an attempt has been made to provide an educational program that meets the needs of students rather than those of teachers and administrators. While most of the teachers have no special training in alternative education, they seem to have a vision of teaching and learning that goes beyond conventional curricula and instruction.

Cooperative and independent approaches to learning are encouraged rather than individual competition. Appropriate rewards are given, and a student's success is not dependent on other students' failure. At Vocational Village, Off-Campus, and Open School grades have been replaced by credits or competency requirements; students are allowed to progress at their own rate toward graduation. At Learning Unlimited, Parkway, and the Environmental Education Program, where grades are given, students are expected to undertake projects and independent study efforts they help design and evaluate. Cooperative learning strategies and a team approach characterize work at the Environmental Education Program. At all three encouragement is given to independent, self-directed learning experiences. Students are offered choices and provided with the instructional support to carry them out.

Sense of community/clear mission. Because these six schools and programs are small and do not attempt to serve everyone, they are able to develop a sense of purpose and a core set of values that are held in common by students and teachers. Each one of the options possesses a cohesiveness and identity that sets it apart from other options and conventional schools. A sense of community and clear mission give meaning to the educational undertaking.

Each school and program concentrates on what it does best rather than trying to be all things to all people. Like private schools, these public schools of choice know who they serve and what they are about. They stand for someone and something. There is general agreement among students and staff about curriculum, instruction, and evaluation. In choosing these options, parents and students have given implied support to their various missions.

Responses to Change

This does not mean that these options have remained static. Times change, and options change with the times. A more conservative climate in the 1980s brought changes to these six schools and programs. Community experiences are now limited and more structured at Parkway and Learning Unlimited than they were ten or twelve years ago. Increased graduation and in-school-hour requirements have limited student curricular choice. Student choice at Open School, particularly in the ELC, is not as great as it once was. A greater amount of prescribed instruction and more time in self-contained rooms is now the rule. Fewer students in the Environmental Education Program are able to have extended experiences as junior zoo keepers, and they cannot roam as freely around the zoo as they once did, because of concerns over increased liability.

While these options have undergone changes, the commitment to alternative public education has remained undiminished in the six school districts represented in this chapter. In fact, one could argue that the changes represent an increased commitment by the districts to meet the changing needs of students as they enter the 1990s. The variety of students served by these options also bears mentioning. Slow and talented, advantaged and disadvantaged benefit from these alternatives. Choice in public education need not be only for a few "special" students. Every student can benefit from an appropriate option.

It must be pointed out, however, that the school districts that offer the alternative schools and programs described in this chapter are, for the most part, large and possess the necessary resources to experiment with a variety of options. What about smaller districts with more modest resources? What options can they afford to offer? While the majority of options described in this chapter serve average to above-average students, what about the at-risk students so prominently mentioned in Chapter 2? What options are available for them? In the next chapter we will look at a modestly financed, medium-sized school district to see what it has done to meet the needs of at-risk students.

FIVE

One Community's Approach to At-Risk Students

Yakima is a community of 50,000 located in the southcentral part of Washington state approximately 150 miles from Seattle and 200 miles from Spokane. It is the political and economic center of the Yakima Valley, one of America's major agricultural areas. Dubbed "the fruit bowl of the nation," the valley is known for its apples and a variety of soft fruits. Not only is Yakima the leading producer of apples in America, it is first in the production of mints and hops. Annual agricultural sales reach $500 million, which puts Yakima among the top dozen or so most productive agricultural counties in the country (Facts about Yakima . . . 1989).

It is an area of contrasts between wealth and poverty. Orchardists, other growers, and professionals who service the agricultural industry are at the social and economic top of the community. Agricultural workers, many of whom are migrant, are at the bottom. Because of its dependence on migrant labor, Yakima has a substantial Hispanic (Mexican-American) population. Indigenous to the valley are Native Americans, primarily of the Yakima tribe, who have a large reservation within Yakima and adjoining counties. Yakima leads Washington state's standard metropolitan statistical areas (SMSAs) in a number of demographic categories. It is first in the percentage of racial minorities, percentage of unemployed, and percentage of families living below the poverty level. It is last in per capita income and the percentage of high school graduates (Yakima Public Schools, 1980).

These characteristics have impacted Yakima's public school system directly. Seventy-one percent of the district's students are white and 29 percent are minority, the latter being overwhelmingly Hispanic. Forty-four percent of the students participate in the federal government's free or reduced-price lunch program. Thirty-seven percent of the students live in single-parent families. All of the school district's elementary schools and three of its four middle schools are designated Chapter 1. In 1987, statewide test results for the total

81

achievement battery placed Yakima twenty-fourth out of the twenty-five largest school districts in Washington. In 1989 the State Office of Superintendent of Public Instruction identified one of Yakima's two high schools as having the highest dropout rate (54 percent) in the state (Nelson, 1989).

A recent development within the city and the county, which has added to the area's woes, has been a dramatic increase in illegal drug-related activity. Yakima has become one of the main distribution points for illegal drugs in the Northwest. In 1988 Yakima's drug problems were featured on a CBS television news report. The use of drugs among the young has increased in recent years, prompting concern among parents and patrons of the public schools. A 1987 survey of Yakima's high school seniors revealed that 60 percent had used marijuana and 25 percent had tried cocaine. These percentages are above the national average for seniors, 50 percent of whom reported marijuana use and 15 percent cocaine use (CLASS Newsletter, 1989).

The Yakima school district has instituted a number of antidrug campaigns and drug education programs. Dealing with students who suffer from substance abuse as well as with the high rate of school dropouts requires more systematic, in-depth effort, however. To meet these challenges, especially the high dropout rate, the school district operates an extensive program of alternative education. Unlike most of the schools and programs described in Chapter 4, Yakima's options are designed almost exclusively to meet the needs of at-risk students.

Participation is by choice. The school district may not require attendance at any of its alternative programs. Alternative education is not seen as a dumping ground for "problem" students but rather as another educational option from which individuals may choose. The district realizes that one model cannot meet the needs of all students and is committed to offering a variety of educational options. According to the district's alternative schools philosophy:

1. Each individual who wishes an education deserves the opportunity to receive one.
2. Each student must be viewed as a worthwhile individual and unique human being.
3. It is a reality that some individual students can function better within an alternative school setting.
4. An alternative educational program needs the flexibility to focus on both the human and academic needs of a student in order to provide the atmosphere for a quality education.

The district's options are located around the city, serving a variety of targeted neighborhoods. With the exception of a main alternative school, the options are small programs serving between twenty-five and seventy-five students. Together, the alternative school and programs enroll more than 500 students, which represents almost 15 percent of the school district's high school population. While not as innovative or "exciting" as the options described in Chapter 4, Yakima's alternative school and programs offer needed services and an effective education to its student clientele, a clientele that is increasing in number each year.

YAKIMA'S ALTERNATIVE SCHOOL AND PROGRAMS

Stanton

Stanton is the largest alternative school in the Yakima school district. Begun in 1971, it was originally called the Upstairs School and was designed to serve only teenage mothers. It later expanded to include any teenage parent; and although it now serves a wide range of students ages 14–20, teenage parents remain its primary focus. Currently 20 percent of the student body is in the teenage parent program. The school enrolls approximately 200 students, 10 percent of whom are minority group members. Many students come from single-parent, low-income homes. Seventy-five percent of the students qualify for the federal government's free or reduced-price lunch program. A number of the older students live on their own and support themselves. The students are extremely mobile. Most have attended several elementary schools. Twenty percent of Stanton's mailings to students' families are regularly returned undelivered because of address changes.

Stanton is located in a vacant elementary school on the far southeast side of town; 1988–89 was its first year at this location. Previously, the option had been housed at another vacant elementary school in the downtown area, but increasing drug-related activity in the downtown and the poor condition of the building necessitated a move. The new location represents a step up in both safety and comfort. The facility is newer and offers sufficient classroom space, a gym, cafeteria, nursery, and library. The neighborhood is more residential and free from drug-related activity.

A complete high school curriculum is offered by a staff of fourteen teachers, a counselor, and principal. The school day runs from 8:00 A.M. to 2:35 P.M. Monday through Thursdays and from 8:00 to 11:55 A.M. on Fridays. Friday afternoon is reserved for student makeup of incomplete work, attendance and discipline violations, faculty meetings, and home visits.

The academic year is divided into six minimesters of six weeks each instead of the twelve-week trimesters that are standard in the district's conventional schools. The purpose of more frequent and shorter grading periods is to assimilate students into the alternative program more easily and to reduce the amount of incomplete and failing work. Conventional district schools report failure for incomplete work and poor attendance every six weeks; failure during a six-week period virtually insures failure for an entire trimester. Students who find themselves in this situation may enroll for a minimester at Stanton and salvage the remainder of the trimester. The shorter grading period is also helpful for students who have difficulty planning and remaining on task for twelve weeks. Dividing the trimester into halves gives them more immediate feedback and more manageable academic goals to consider. The minimester format is used in all the district's alternative programs.

The school day is divided into seven periods (six of fifty minutes and one of thirty minutes). In the fifty-minute periods traditional subjects, such as world history, algebra, business education, reading, art, physical education, and general science, are taught. During the thirty-minute period all students participate in a course titled "Family." Here they meet in small groups with their teacher/advisor to develop friendships within a small-group setting and to focus on interdisciplinary skills, leadership training, and self-esteem building. The emphasis in "Family" is on affective education and personal growth.

Establishing personal relationships with students and meeting individual needs is an expectation of teachers at Stanton and of all teachers in the district's alternative programs. Their role is that of a teacher/counselor who is responsible for both the cognitive and affective needs in students' education. Class size is kept relatively small (sixteen to eighteen) to facilitate the teacher/counselor role.

Instruction in the regular courses is primarily whole-class and teacher-directed. There is some individualized work, particularly in reading and creative writing, but in most classes students work and progress at the same rate through the course material. The curriculum emphasizes basic skills acquisition and general knowledge. Students who want specialized vocational or advanced academic coursework must take those subjects at the regional skills center or at either of the district's two conventional high schools. Approximately 5 percent of Stanton's students are dual enrolled in either the skills center or a conventional school. Students earn letter grades for completed work and upon successful completion receive a high school diploma from one of the two conventional high schools. An 80 percent attendance rate is required for the granting of credit. Students who are deficient may make up attendance on Friday afternoons. Daily attendance averages a little over 60 percent.

Because the clientele at Stanton has specific needs and the option has been established to meet those needs, additional coursework is available in parenting, substance abuse, and the law. Seventy-five percent of Stanton's students are or have been involved in drug and alcohol abuse. A support group is offered for students trying to end their dependence, and the school works closely with a number of social agencies to obtain outpatient help for students with medical and emotional problems. All of the school's teachers have undergone training in alcohol and drug awareness and are competent to serve as counselors.

Most of Stanton's students need money and work to support themselves and their families. As a concession, the school allows students to earn up to seven elective credits for job-related activities. Students must show their paystubs and obtain documentation of their work from their employers. These elective credits may not be used to satisfy academic or vocational requirements, but they do reduce the overall credit burden, which can be formidable for many of these students. This option is available to all students in the district's alternative programs.

Stanton provides a program for homebound students who are unable to attend school. Most of these students are recent mothers, but also included are students with transportation problems or full-time work schedules that make attending school impossible. A teacher trained in early childhood education makes weekly visits to the mothers' homes to bring school work and to educate them about the nutritional, hygienic, and intellectual needs of their babies. All homebound students complete required school work through contracts that are assigned and corrected by two contract teachers at school.

Contracted learning is also available for students who attend school on a part-time basis. The contract teachers work with these students and their subject-matter teachers to put together temporary programs of study. Part-time students include teenage parents who are on the waiting list for full-time use of one of the twelve cribs in the school's nursery. Seniors receive preference for full-time use, but some in the lower grades are assigned morning or afternoon use.

Students who are a few credits shy of graduating comprise another group of part-timers. Interestingly, a few of these are middle-aged individuals trying to obtain their high school diploma many years after leaving school. They include a divorced 40-year-old mother with limited prospects who realizes she needs to obtain her diploma to become economically independent, and a serviceman near retirement who has learned that a prerequisite to earning his final stripe is a high school diploma. These individuals come to school one hour a week for each credit they are working on. They meet with one of the two contract teachers to have work evaluated and to receive new assignments. Another option for students is the General Education Development (GED). Two GED study periods a day are offered for older students who have too many credits to complete for a regular high school diploma. Weekly tests for the GED are scheduled for students who are ready to take them. In 1988–89, Stanton certified approximately 200 students for the GED. Stanton is having a positive effect on the students it serves. In 1987–88, forty-four students earned high school diplomas; in 1988–89 the number was 68. The trend was expected to increase in 1989–90.

The Place

The second largest alternative program offered by the Yakima school district is the Yakima Learning Center, or "The Place," as it is more commonly called. Originally begun in 1968, the program is funded and operated jointly by the Yakima school district and the Washington State Division of Juvenile Rehabilitation (DJR). The district provides the teachers and curriculum materials and DJR provides the facility, transportation, and supplies. The Place is one of six state learning centers operated by DJR. Other learning centers are located in Seattle, Tacoma, Spokane, Everett, and Walla Walla.

The Place is located in an excellent new facility six blocks west of downtown. It features four classrooms, a science lab, a woodshop, an arts and crafts room, a library, a game room, a universal gym, and a locker room and showers. The program serves seventy to seventy-five students ages 15–20, three-fourths of whom are male. Approximately 12 percent of the students are minority.

Most students have had contact with the law. Students on parole or probation are given priority and constitute 75 percent of the program's enrollment. These individuals have either been committed to an institution, placed in a group home, or are living at home while fulfilling a community service requirement. The program's two vans are used to transport students from a variety of locations to attend The Place. The 25 percent of nonadjudicated students are young people with personal or academic problems that have kept them from being successful in regular schools. Virtually all of the students at The Place come from economically disadvantaged homes. Ninety percent qualify for the federal government's free or reduced-price lunch program. A free breakfast program, instituted in the fall of 1988, provides an additional meal for students.

The Place is administered by a program director employed by DJR. She oversees six teachers, three counselors, and one instructional aide, who together offer a complete high school curriculum. The school day is virtually identical to that of Stanton's. Students attend six forty-five-minute periods from 8:00 A.M. to 2:10 P.M. Monday through Thursday and a shorter schedule from 8:00 to 11:45 A.M. on Friday. As at Stanton, Friday afternoons are used for makeup of incomplete work, attendance and discipline violations, and faculty meetings. The six-week minimester grading period is used. Students earn letter grades and work toward a diploma to be awarded by either one of the two conventional high schools. There is no GED option.

The course offerings are similar to those at Stanton. Students who wish to take advanced academic or specialized vocational courses may attend the conventional high schools or the regional skills center. Approximately 10 percent of the students take advantage of this option. Contract and independent work are available for students who are unable to attend The Place full time. Students with full- or part-time jobs, teenage parents, and mothers-to-be are the typical contract students and make up 10 percent of the enrollment.

Contract students come in weekly to have work reviewed and to receive new assignments. A contract teacher assists these students as well as other students who are not enrolled at The Place. The other students are similar to those doing contract work at Stanton. They are beyond school age and have only a few credits remaining before obtaining their high school diploma. As at Stanton, students may receive up to seven elective credits for job-related activities. Attendance is required, but the 80 percent rate at Stanton is not enforced at The Place. Instead, a class called "Second Chance" is offered for absentees. Students who enroll in "Second Chance" and complete its requirements may receive full credit for partial work done in the previous minimester.

Instruction is completely individualized. Students are at various levels of ability and at various stages of high school completion. State funding keeps the student teacher ratio at ten-to-one. Students work in materials appropriate for their ability level and at their own rate. Most students are performing two to three years below grade level. The program is not without its academically able, however. A number of students are considerably above average in ability but are underachievers. Their problem is motivation and behavior.

As at Stanton, a daily thirty-minute period called "Family" is part of the school day. A group of nine to ten students meets with a teacher to develop friendships, discuss matters of personal interest, and plan special projects and community service activities. The teacher's role in "Family" is that of counselor or facilitator, and the agenda is often open-ended to take advantage of student needs and concerns. A substantial amount of group counseling occurs in "Family."

Substance abuse is a serious problem among students. Approximately 90 percent of the students have experienced or are experiencing substance abuse. All but one of the teachers have been trained in substance abuse awareness, and all are expected to counsel students who are having problems with dependency. Teachers meet weekly with a drug and alcohol consultant to discuss various students and their substance abuse problems. If necessary, they refer students to various social agencies and contracted services. A weekly student support group meets with one of the teachers who is also a certified drug and alcohol counselor. To aid in drug detection, The Place has bought a drug testing kit manufactured by Abbott Laboratories. Students may volunteer to undergo confidential testing (students under court order must submit to compulsory testing) to monitor their progress in ending their dependency. Clean test results have proven an excellent way for some successful students to assure skeptical parents that they are clean.

Progress toward increased attendance and high school graduation has been slow but steady. Average daily attendance in 1988–89 was 60 percent. While this percentage may not seem impressive, it reflects considerable improvement over these same students' attendance at conventional schools. A 1986 study conducted by the director found that students at The Place increased their attendance by a third over what it had been at conventional schools. In 1987, eleven students earned high school diplomas; in 1988, four; and in 1989, nine. Numbers do not tell the whole story, however. They do not tell us, for example, of the young man who was convicted of armed robbery, sentenced, and eventually paroled to The Place. Upon discharge he decided to continue his studies, graduated, and is now enrolled in the local community college majoring in law enforcement. His goal is to become a policeman.

Key/OIC

The Key/OIC program operates out of a facility leased by the Opportunities Industrialization Center (OIC) on the far north side of town. Yakima's OIC is part of a national organization that operates adult education and job-training programs funded by federal grants. The district rents one large and one small classroom from OIC for its two full-time teachers (one male and one female), one instructional aide, and forty to forty-five students. The student body is more ethnically diverse than at Stanton or The Place. Approximately 65 percent of the students are white and 35 percent are minority. As in the other alternative programs, most of the students come from economically disadvantaged homes. Over 90 percent qualify for the free or reduced-price lunch program. Ten percent of the students are teenage parents.

Students are attracted to Key/OIC because it is smaller than Stanton or The Place and adjusting to two teachers is easier than dealing with six or fourteen. Most of the students have been involved with drugs and choose this location to remove themselves from the peer group and temptations that led to their substance abuse. The teachers at Key/OIC will not tolerate students using or being under the influence of drugs. Students engaging in drug-related activities are dropped from the program, no exceptions. These students are referred to Stanton or The Place, where counseling and support groups are available for substance abusers.

Students are also attracted to the program because of its cooperative arrangement with OIC. Qualified students may enroll part-time in clerical or sales classes offered at OIC while attending the alternative academic program the remainder of the time. Individuals enrolled in the clerical and sales programs receive an hourly wage of $3.35. About 20 percent of the students participate in this cooperative arrangement. Students who live in the neighborhood near the OIC facility find it convenient to attend school there.

The school day is divided into six periods that begin at 8:00 A.M. and end at 2:15 P.M. Like Stanton and The Place, students attend school Monday through Thursday all day and half day on Fridays. First period consists of the two teachers teaming to assist students working on contracts and independent work in science and math. Second period is again teamed, but with all students working on reading and language arts in a whole-class format. Third and fourth period the teachers alternate between social studies and "Family." The content of "Family" at Key/OIC is different from that at Stanton and The Place. Teachers spend less time on affective education and counseling. Instead, such topics as first aid, health, civics, the law, and AIDS are covered. After lunch is fifth period and another teamed class, this time in art. Students work on ceramic chalking, drawing, and calligraphy. Fifth period is clearly the most popular class at Key/OIC. It is so popular that the teachers require students to be passing four subjects and to have an 80 percent attendance rate before they may enroll in art. Sixth period is divided into art again and to individual studies. Students who are behind in work or need remediation in language arts, reading, or vocabulary work with one of the teachers on individual contracts and independent study. As at Stanton and The Place, students receive letter grades for their work.

Similar options exist at Key/OIC as at other alternative programs: Students may earn elective credits for job-related activities; students needing advanced academic or specialized technical courses may enroll at conventional high schools or at the regional skills center. Currently 10 percent of the students take advantage of the dual enrollment option. A third available option is a half day of school and a half day of work. A number of the students support themselves and must work full or part time. They take classes at Key/OIC either in the morning or the afternoon and do independent contracted work at home on their own time. Currently, about 10 percent are doing this.

Key/OIC was originally designed as a transition program for students ages 14–21. After a limited stay, students were to transfer to Stanton and eventually to one of the conventional high schools. However, students have been reluctant to leave, and over time Key/OIC has become a long-term program that offers the classes necessary to obtain a high school diploma. Most of the students have academic deficiencies. As a group, they perform several years below grade level. Ten percent of the students, however, are above average. They include an overweight girl who dropped out of a conventional high school because she was being harassed and ridiculed. Another girl, an honor student, had moved to Yakima from a small rural high school. She initially enrolled in one of the district's conventional high schools but could not adjust to its size and the number of students and so dropped out.

Key/OIC is having modest success with its students. Average daily attendance is 65 percent. The granting of high school diplomas has increased steadily, if slowly. In 1988, three students graduated; in

1989, six. An occasional individual decides to pursue education beyond high school. In 1988, one graduate received a scholarship to attend South Seattle Community College's aviation mechanic program. In 1989, another graduate enrolled in a well respected automotive and truck technical school in Phoenix, Arizona.

Project 107

Six blocks east of downtown, just behind the Greyhound bus station, is a modest two-story wooden frame house that serves as the home of Project 107. The school district rents a large classroom, a small study room, a kitchen, and a bathroom on the first floor of the house. A foster home placement service and a community outreach program share the remainder of the first floor and all of the second.

Begun in 1985, Project 107 serves street kids ages 14–20 who have no extended family and unsatisfactory living conditions. All of the students are welfare recipients and qualify for the federal government's free or reduced-price lunch program. All have experienced or are experiencing substance abuse. Five percent of the students are minority. Virtually all of the students live in the surrounding neighborhood and will not leave it to attend school. All have either dropped out or been kicked out of conventional schools. There is an equal number of males and females. Half of the females are either mothers or mothers-to-be.

Like Key/OIC, Project 107 was originally designed as a transition program. It was a program for reentering students who needed to experience success and gain basic academic skills before transferring to one of the other alternative programs or one of the conventional high schools in the district. One teacher worked with approximately thirty students on remedial math, English, social studies, and science. Half of the students attended a three-hour session in the morning (8:30 to 11:30 A.M.) and the other half, a three-hour session in the afternoon (11:30 A.M. to 2:30 P.M.). Each session consisted of three fifty-minute periods with ten minute breaks between. Given their previous unsuccessful experiences with public schools, half a day was about all these students could handle.

Today the program is still divided into two three-hour sessions, one in the morning and another in the afternoon, but now almost half of the students attend both sessions. Enrollment has grown to forty, and a second teacher with training in math and science has been assigned to the morning session to assist the full-time teacher, who is trained in English and social studies. Twenty-four students are currently enrolled for the morning session; eleven of those continue into the afternoon, joined by five new students for a total of sixteen. Some students do transfer to one of the other alternative programs or conventional high schools, but very few—only about 10 percent. Most students choose to remain at Project 107 to complete their high school course requirements or prepare for the GED. Students with specialized interests may enroll at one of the other options, the skills center, or at one of the conventional high schools to obtain the necessary class or classes.

Upon entry to Project 107, students are given diagnostic tests in math, reading, writing, and language arts. Results indicate that, on average, students are performing two to four years below grade level. They are then placed at the appropriate levels in various subjects and assigned skills books and teacher-made materials. Students work quietly on their own at large tables and receive periodic assistance from their teacher(s).

All work is given letter grades, and an 80 percent attendance rate is required to receive credit. Students work toward either a GED or a high school diploma granted by one of the two conventional high schools. As in all the alternative programs, the option to do contracted independent study is available. At Project 107 three kinds of students may qualify for independent study: mothers or mothers-to-be, the seriously ill, and those working over twenty-five hours a week. These students check in weekly to obtain new work and to receive evaluation of completed assignments. In addition, all students may receive elective credits for job-related activities, as is the case in all the alternative programs.

Appropriate behavior is expected and enforced. Posted on the wall are five rules all students must follow:

Do not come to class wasted
No smoking in the building
Respect others
No lying or cheating
No swearing

First-time violation of any of these five rules results in a one-day suspension from the program. A second violation can result in a longer suspension or some other form of punishment. Most of these students have a history of behavior problems, which have in large part, contributed to their lack of success in conventional schools. As a result, punishments are handled on a case-by-case basis and may

vary considerably for different students. The most effective punishment is the threat of removal from the program. Students at Project
107 are there by choice, and don't want to leave. Most of these students have less than satisfactory home lives and have come to depend
on the structure and guidance they receive from the program and the
teacher(s). A particularly strong bond exists between the students
and the full-time teacher, a thirtyish male who has shared some of
their life experiences. They know he is available at night and on week-
ends to assist them with personal problems. His service to them does
not end at 2:30 P.M. on Friday.

Enrollment has grown steadily during the past three years. Dropping out and absenteeism continue at Project 107, but progress is
being made. Average daily attendance was 57 percent in 1987–88 and
increased to 68 percent in 1988–89. Completion rates are showing
modest improvements as well. In 1988 one student earned a high
school diploma and two received their GEDs. In 1989 three earned
diplomas and one received a GED. Currently, half of the students
have remained enrolled for two years, a testimony to the program's
holding power.

Outreach

Three blocks from The Place is a small red brick building across
the street from the Albertson's Supermarket. The four-room, one-
story structure had seen duty as both a radio station and church, but
since 1979 it has housed the district's Outreach alternative program.
A subprogram of the Yakima Learning Center, Outreach is designed
to serve twenty-four of the most difficult students in the Yakima
school district. The typical Outreach student is angry, hostile, adjudicated, economically disadvantaged, and between the ages of 14 and
21. Virtually all of Outreach's students have experienced or are experiencing problems with substance abuse. Ninety percent qualify for
the federal government's free or reduced-price lunch program. Fifteen percent are minority and 75 percent are male.

The offenses of these students are many and varied. They include
burning down one of the district's elementary schools, injuring a policeman in a car chase, dealing drugs, and beating up the director of a
drug rehabilitation program. The cause of most of the offenses can be
found in unsatisfactory home lives. Virtually all of the students come
from single-parent families. Twenty percent live in group homes.

The emphasis at Outreach is on developing affective skills first
and cognitive skills second. Affective objectives of the program in-

clude working together cooperatively, using acceptable language in social settings, demonstrating appropriate behavior in public places, and building personal confidence and self-esteem. Cognitive objectives include basic skills acquisition in math and English, primarily in computation and reading comprehension. To accomplish these objectives, Outreach's curriculum is a combination of in-school academic coursework and outdoor environmental education. Students spend approximately three days a week in school and two days a week away from school.

Outreach's staff consists of one teacher, an athletic middle-aged male who has taught in the program since its inception in 1979. He commands the students' respect because of his knowledge and skill in outdoor education and his commitment to alternative education. Prior to this assignment he taught in another district alternative program for five years. Originally trained as a physical education and recreation teacher, he has had experience as a YMCA physical fitness director and summer camp director. He is assisted by a female instructional aide who has been with the program for four years.

In school, students pursue academic subjects during a six-period day that starts at 8:00 A.M. and ends at 2:00 P.M. The daily schedule begins with English from 8:00 to 8:50 A.M. During this time students work on writing, spelling, and vocabulary. Students are divided into two groups that reflect ability levels. One group works with the teacher and another with the instructional aide. After a ten-minute break, science follows from 9:00 to 9:50 A.M. Here students work on group lessons and individual assignments. Another ten-minute break, and math is next. Work in math is totally individualized. From 10:55 to 11:30 A.M. the students and teacher engage in discussions about matters of personal concern, current events, interpersonal skills, and trip planning. Lunch follows from 11:30 A.M. to 12:30 P.M. Silent sustained reading is from 12:30 to 1:00 P.M. followed by physical education, the last period of the day from 1:00 to 2:00 P.M. A nearby park serves as the athletic field for softball, soccer, and volleyball games.

The two days a week of outdoor education are spent camping out at a variety of locations around Washington state. Most trips are three-day, two-night affairs, which means students and teachers are on the road two out of every three weeks. Trips in the winter are fewer than in the fall and spring. Trip destinations include Westport and Grays Harbor on the Olympic peninsula, the San Juan Islands in Puget Sound, Vancouver and Victoria in British Columbia, the Oregon coast, Mount Rainier, Chinook Pass and other locations in the

Cascade Mountains, and numerous sites in and near the Yakima Valley. Two vans supplied by The Place alternative program are the means of transportation.

Activities at the different destinations vary. On the Washington and Oregon coasts, students fish, crab, and engage in whale watching. In the Cascades, hiking and backpacking are the main activities. In the Yakima Valley historical and cultural sites are the focus. Occasionally, longer, more involved trips are planned. In 1986 the students took a four-day excursion to Vancouver, British Columbia, to see EXPO. In 1988 the class spent five days at Grays Harbor cleaning birds and beaches that had been soiled by an oil tanker spill off the coast. In 1989 the most ambitious trip was undertaken, a twelve-day expedition to San Diego, Los Angeles, and San Francisco.

These trips are designed to serve a number of purposes in the education of Outreach's students. First, they remove students for a short time from negative environments and peer groups. The trips allow individuals to experience new settings and different groups of people. Second, traveling and living together with a small number of individuals can lead to friendships, which are all too few among Outreach students. Third, students are exposed to a positive male role model, something most have not experienced in their lives. Ninety percent of the students are missing their fathers, and for the boys this can be particularly detrimental to healthy character formation. Fourth, students must expend some energy and demonstrate some physical fitness on these outings. Most of Outreach's students have avoided exercise. Many are ashamed of their bodies and their personal appearance. Exercise and the accomplishment of outdoor skills help to build confidence and pride. Fifth, while on trips students must interact with the public in such social settings as restaurants, museums, and theaters. They are forced to practice interpersonal skills that will help them be more socially effective in later life. Finally, students learn about the environment and their place in it. They gather information that is reviewed and studied when they return to Yakima and take up their classroom work. Learning takes on more immediacy and meaning when it can be related to personal, real life experiences.

An added lesson from these trips results from the fact that students must earn money and assist in the planning. The program's main source of revenue is the cutting and selling of firewood. A great deal of time is spent in the fall cutting and delivering firewood for sale. Getting students to plan trips is not a easy task. Many students resist responsibility, and it takes patient guidance by the teacher to get them to assume it. By spring, however, students are finally able to undertake trip planning from beginning to end by themselves.

Students must demonstrate responsible behavior and the necessary outdoor skills before they are allowed to participate in the out-of-school excursions. The school district owns a camp near White Pass, some fifty miles from Yakima, where Outreach students can learn how to pitch tents, cook meals, and pack up belongings. Students must earn the right to take each trip by demonstrating acceptable behavior while in school and on past trips. Points are accumulated between trips, and only those who accumulate the required number of points may go. Maintaining acceptable attendance is a prerequisite for participation in trips.

In addition to the special features of the program, Outreach offers most of the options available in Yakima's other alternative school and programs. Students may earn elective credits for job-related experiences. Students may also do contracted independent work to make up for lost time or to accelerate progress. Approximately 10 percent of Outreach's students work full time and take advantage of independent contracted work. As is the case with all the alternative programs, Outreach students may dual enroll at the skills center or at either of the two conventional high schools; however, very few do.

Conceived as a transition program, Outreach is finding, as the other alternative programs have found, that students are reluctant to transfer back to the conventional high schools or even to Stanton. The average stay at Outreach has grown from one to two years. Students are electing to complete their high school requirements at Outreach or take their GED after leaving the program. Outreach does not have its own GED program.

Daily attendance is very good at Outreach, averaging 67 percent, second best among the district's alternative programs. In 1988 the program had one graduate and in 1989 two who received their high school diplomas. Over the past few years three of Outreach's students have continued their education beyond high school. One girl enrolled in a small Bible college in Oregon and is completing her studies. Two boys attended the Divers Institute in Seattle and are now professional divers, one in Scotland, the other in Seattle.

Stride

Begun in 1986, Stride is the school district's newest alternative program. It is located in the Southeast Community Center, not far from the county fairgrounds on the far southeast side of Yakima. The neighborhood is predominantly minority, mainly black and Hispanic. The Southeast Community Center is a large, concrete building that serves as a social service agency for the surrounding neighborhood. In the building are housed a health clinic, legal services and welfare offices, and afterschool youth programs. The school district rents one large and one small room to house the alternative program.

Stride has a minority enrollment of 80 percent, highest of all the alternative programs. This is in large part because of the program's location, but it is also due to its teacher, an African-American who relates well to minority students and has considerable experience (nine years) in and commitment to alternative education. His previous assignment was at Key/OIC, where he spent two years. His sister is now one of the two Key/OIC teachers. The profile of the student body at Stride is similar to that of the other alternative programs. Most of the thirty students are economically disadvantaged, and virtually all qualify for the federal government's free or reduced-price lunch program. Ninety percent have experienced or are experiencing some form of drug abuse. Fifty percent are adjudicated. They range in age from 14 to 20, but most are in the 14–15 age range, giving Stride a younger student body than the other alternative programs.

The teacher and a part-time instructional aide run the program, which operates Monday through Thursday from 8:00 A.M. to 2:35 P.M. and on Friday from 8:00 to 11:30 A.M. As with the other alternative programs, Friday afternoon is for student makeup of incomplete work, attendance and discipline violations, faculty meetings and home visits. The school day consists of six periods. First period is math/science from 8:00 to 8:55 A.M. Students work individually with workbooks and teacher-made materials and are assisted by the teacher. Second period is social studies from 9:00 to 9:55 A.M. Here whole-class instruction by the teacher, a social studies major, is the rule. Third period is life skills, from 10:00 to 10:55 A.M. Again, whole-class instruction is the approach. Topics such as abuse, AIDS, the law, interpersonal relationships, and job-related skills are covered at this time. After lunch is fourth period, reading/language arts. Depending on the lesson, students work individually or together as a class. Grammar and writing exercises are done individually, while discussions of literature are whole class. Fifth period is ethnic studies, from 12:45 to 1:35 P.M. Mexican-American and African-American history and culture are stressed, and instruction varies from whole-class to individual assignments. Last period is physical education, from 1:40 to 2:35 P.M. The community center has an excellent gym, which students use for basketball and volleyball games. An adjoining weight room offers another opportunity for physical fitness. Softball is played outdoors at a nearby park.

Most of the students are performing below district norms academically; two years below grade level is the average. Each student is diagnosed informally and assigned the appropriate materials. Acquisition of basic skills is the focus of the curriculum at Stride. Designed as a transition program, it is hoped that students will transfer to Stanton or one of the conventional high schools after receiving the necessary remediation. The reality is that these students, like the students in the other alternative programs, are becoming comfortable at Stride and are unlikely to transfer. Currently none take advantage of the dual enrollment option; only one has transferred to Stanton, and none to either of the conventional high schools.

As is the case at the other alternative programs, Stride students may earn elective credits for job-related activities. They may also do contracted independent work to make up for lost time or to accelerate progress. Approximately 20 percent of Stride's students attend the program part-time and fulfill the remaining requirements through independent contracted work.

The current teacher was assigned to the program in 1988 to give it purpose and stability. He spent much of 1988–89 getting it back on track. In its first two years Stride had had two different teachers and suffered from a lack of purpose and continuity. Average daily attendance was below 50 percent. The younger age of the students provided an added challenge, since their maturity level was lower than that of students in the other programs.

Slowly but steadily the program has begun to turn around. Average daily attendance has increased to 55 percent, still lowest among the district's alternative programs but an improvement over the previous years. In 1988, there were no high school graduates from Stride, but in 1989 there were three. With a cohort of 14- and 15-year-olds in their second year, Stride's future graduation rates look bright. The District is planning to expand the program in both the 1989–90 and 1990–91 school years.

CONCLUSIONS

Yakima's extensive alternative education program shares the characteristics of the exemplary schools and programs described in Chapter 4. They are: smallness, concern for the whole student, supportive environment, and sense of community/clear mission. While

Yakima's alternative program is generally effective, it is not perfect. Weaknesses as well as strengths can be found in the program.

Meeting the Effectiveness Criteria

Smallness. If small is better, then Yakima's alternative program is one of the best. Enrollment at the six sites ranges from a low of twenty-four students at Outreach to a high of 200 at Stanton. Outreach and Stride are virtually one-room school houses, while Key/OIC and Project 107 are two-teacher operations. Stanton, the largest with 200 students, is a very small comprehensive high school. Because of its smallness, there is little opportunity for a student to "fall between the cracks" in the district's alternative program.

Concern for the whole student. Students who enroll in the alternative education program receive a great deal of personal attention. The teacher-student ratio is smaller than that of the conventional schools. Classes like "Family" increase the chances that students will develop personal relationships with a teacher and other students. Alternative teachers serve as counselors as well as instructors. They are expected to take an interest in the problems of their students and assist them in finding solutions to matters of personal concern. The emotional rehabilitation of individuals is the major focus of teachers, and they do their job well.

Supportive environment. The program's main strength lies in providing services for its student clientele. Drug testing and counseling are available for substance abusers, daycare for teenage parents, and contracted independent learning for the employed. A variety of options have been made available at a number of neighborhood locations to make taking advantage of the services easier. Many of the students are reluctant to leave their neighborhoods. Locating schools around town allows students to attend programs on their own "turf."

Sense of community/clear mission. Most of the students served by the alternative program have economic and emotional problems that must be dealt with before they can pursue a substantive academic curriculum. As Abraham Maslow (1970) has reminded us, it is difficult to become self-actualized before satisfying more basic needs such as safety, love and belonging, and self-esteem. Yakima's alternative program is in the business of emotional and psychological rehabilitation, and that is why it concentrates so much effort on the services it provides to its student clientele.

Recent research of effective alternative schools indicates that Yakima's emphasis on the social-psychological aspects of schooling is not misplaced. In a study of fourteen special schools and programs designed for at-risk students, Gary Wehlage and colleagues (1989) found that concentration on student self-esteem, personal problems of students, and connecting school to the outside lives of students were key ingredients of school and program effectiveness. They also observed that these schools and programs were not satisfied simply to create a positive social-psychological climate. The effective schools found ways to demand student performance within a supportive context. This expectation of student performance is an important one. A study of at-risk students by Sandra Miller and colleagues (1988) found that excessive accommodation of students limited academic engagement and the overall usefulness of the program. While it was important to be accommodating and understanding of at-risk students' needs, teachers and administrators must be careful to hold students accountable to some standards of behavior and academic performance.

Weaknesses

The major weakness of Yakima's alternative program is its academic curriculum. Even at Stanton, with its fourteen teachers and comprehensive course of study, students are not receiving an academic education comparable to the one offered at the conventional high schools in the district. At Key/OIC and Project 107 with two teachers, and Outreach and Stride with one, the disparity between the conventional and alternative academic curricula is even greater. No matter how intelligent and well trained, a single teacher or even two cannot deliver a comprehensive high school curriculum to students. As a result, some compromising takes place. General science is substituted for biology, pre-algebra for algebra, social studies for U.S. history, and elementary stories for senior English.

While part of the problem is delivery of a substantive academic curriculum, another part of the problem is the students' level of ability and their willingness to master such a curriculum. The alternative school and programs in Yakima are attracting students who are generally performing below district norms, not just by a year or two but by several years in many cases. Would these students take advantage of a comprehensive academic curriculum if it were offered to them? It is doubtful. Virtually all failed at such a curriculum while enrolled in their conventional schools, and they are reluctant to return to it or the conventional school even on a part-time basis. As noted, very few of the alternative students take advantage of the dual enrollment option that is available to them.

While part of the reluctance to return is the unwillingness to compete academically, an additional reason is the inability of alternative students to compete socially with their peers. In most high schools, as in our larger society, status and social acceptance are determined in part by what one owns and wears. Most of Yakima's alternative students are poor. They cannot afford nice clothes and costly possessions. When asked why she would not return to her conventional high school, one alternative student replied, "I can't compete with the other students in the fashion parade." Poor students thus have an added barrier to overcome to achieve acceptance by their peers.

Strengths

Yakima's alternative program has had its share of academic success, however. Graduation and attendance rates of at-risk students are increasing modestly but steadily. A few alternative students go on to postsecondary education, and enrollment in the programs is on the rise. But are these the criteria that give us a true measure of an alternative program's success? Do they tell us about the 14-year-old girl who sat on top of a garage shouting obscenities and refusing to come down; or the 16-year-old boy who drove to the alternative school but remained in his car, too shy to leave it; or the teenage mother expecting her second child and despairing of her situation? These individuals were encouraged to enroll in the alternative program. They were shown patience and caring by dedicated teachers and provided with the necessary assistance to allow them to come down from the garage, leave the car, and regain the hope and desire to try once again. They learned to see themselves positively. They were able to acquire the basic skills necessary to obtain jobs and become meaningful participants in society. They are the true success stories of Yakima's alternative education program and the justification for its continued existence.

A college scholarship application letter written by an alternative school graduate reveals the positive impact the program had on her life:

Three years ago I dropped out of high school because of an unplanned pregnancy. Receiving a diploma, not to mention a college education, seemed an impossible goal. After having my

daughter, a friend encouraged me to attend _____; that would
enable me to go to school and have my daughter in a day care
where I could participate and interact with her and the other
children.

I tried school half-heartedly, but then realized I was enjoy-
ing myself and learning at the same time. This encouraged me to
work harder and attend regularly. At _____ we are taught to respect ourselves and others, no matter what our race, age, or
color. It is based upon positive self-awareness, which is something I lacked before attending _____. Since then I have met
many goals, and I am regularly meeting new ones. My self-
confidence and my daughter's has grown 100 percent.

When I came back to school, I found that I was well suited
to the field of business English and business law. With so many
courses available to me, these skills have readied me for the
business world; they have opened many career doors for me.

To further my business education, I volunteered to work as
a secretarial assistant at the General Services Administration. I
am learning skills in the classroom and on the job that will be
needed in my business career.

The benefit of being able to learn and work in an atmosphere which relates to the kind of career I am striving for is in-
valuable. Alternative education has enabled me to earn a diploma while learning vocational skills. Because _____ is small,
the students are able to work with teachers on a one-to-one basis, which has helped me to boost my self-confidence. The
teachers have taught me how to make any task an interesting
learning experience. This kind of education has given me the
chance to work closely with the daycare staff and learn valuable
parenting skills, along with learning how to be a wise consumer.
Because of _____'s flexible scheduling, I am able to attend
school and work part-time.

My education, since joining the student body of _____ has
been very enjoyable, hard work. I believe it has helped me to
make my daughter and me better people.

Now that I have conquered the goal of graduating, I hope to
reach my next goal of a college education. I plan to attend the
summer quarter at _____ Community College this June. There I
will major in business and minor in psychology. Although I
would like to attend college full time after graduation, my financial position prohibits me from doing so. I shall be working full
time and would like to attend night courses at the college. I am

anxious to learn more and further my education after high school. It would allow me to expand my skills and knowledge, as well as provide a secure future for my family.

I hope you find me a suitable candidate. I am very proud to be a graduate of an alternative school and would be honored to receive your scholarship.

Yakima's satisfaction with its alternative education program has led the district to consider options within two of its conventional schools. With the 1989–90 school year, Yakima began offering magnet programs at one elementary and one middle school. The programs offered are computing, Spanish language immersion, and gifted and talented classes. With a new superintendent supportive of the magnet schools concept, Yakima appears committed to expanding options within its public schools.

The social, economic, and educational problems facing Yakima are not unique. Drugs, poverty, and high student dropout rates are matters of national concern. Public schools throughout America are being asked to provide solutions to these problems. One solution schools are trying is the introduction of options and choice that attempt to meet not only students' cognitive needs but their social and psychological needs as well. What role can alternative schools and programs play in reducing social and economic inequality? And what about meeting the needs of highly motivated and academically able students dissatisfied with the education they are receiving? Can public schools of choice help to meet their needs as well? What does the future hold for public alternative education as we move into the 1990s? Answers to these and other questions are the focus of the next and last chapter.

SIX

The Future of Public Alternative Education

There are signs that America is becoming a more divided society: over the last decade, the rich have been getting richer; the poor have been getting more numerous, and those in the middle do not appear to be doing as well as they used to. If America is "coming back," as President Reagan reassured us in the wake of the economic malaise of the early 1980s, it may be coming back in a harsh and alien form. (Ehrenreich, 1986, p. 44)

A DIVIDED AMERICA

America in the 1990s finds itself becoming a society increasingly divided into haves and have-nots. According to Congress's Joint Economic Committee, the wealthiest 20 percent of Americans increased their share of the nation's income from 40 percent in 1967 to 43 percent in 1984. During that same period, the share of national income for the country's poorest 20 percent decreased from 6 to 5 percent (Middle Class Squeeze, 1986). While the 1980s proved to be a difficult decade for many Americans, it was especially hard on the poor. According to the William T. Grant Foundation Commission on Work, Family and Citizenship (1988), young male high school graduates earned 28 percent less in constant dollars in 1986 than they did in 1973. For young male high school dropouts, the decline in constant dollars during that period was 42 percent.

The decline in America's manufacturing and heavy industry sectors over the last fifteen to twenty years has reduced the number of relatively high-paying manual and unskilled jobs. They have been replaced by lower-paying jobs, primarily in the service sector. While unemployment rates dropped during the 1980s, those employed have found it more difficult to support themselves and their families on the wages they earn. In 1973, 60 percent of all employed young males earned enough money to support a three-person family. By 1985, the percentage had dropped to 44 percent (William T. Grant Fdn., 1988).

America's economic restructuring has meant job displacement for millions of Americans, especially those in areas where factories have been traditionally located. Most affected by the changes have been the less advantaged and less mobile members of our society. As James Comer (1985) observed:

> In the face of this change and uncertainty, all American families have experienced stress. Drug abuse, an epidemic level of mental health problems, unacceptable crime rates, and a number of other social indicators apparent across the socioeconomic spectrum attest to this fact. But the most adversely affected of all are those groups whose members were closed out of the political and economic main-stream of society before science and technology drastically changed the nature of work. (p. 247)

The social indicators to which Comer refers are disturbing. Today, 25 percent of school-age children live in poverty. Twenty percent of all children live with a single parent. Fifteen percent have teenage parents, and 10 percent have parents who are illiterate. Since 1960, teenage drug use has risen 6,000 percent, teenage homicides 200 percent, delinquency 130 percent, and teenage pregnancy more than 100 percent (Haberman, 1988). In 1965, 15 percent of teenage girls who gave birth were not married. Today, more than 50 percent are unwed, and 19 percent of all children in America are born illegitimate (London, 1987).

These statistics are even more troubling when one realizes their negative relationship to school performance, retention, and eventual economic well-being. A 1986 poll conducted by Louis Harris and Associates for Planned Parenthood revealed that teenagers who were sexually active had lower average grades in school than sexually inactive teenagers (McClellan, 1987). According to a study by the National Research Council (1987), children of teenage parents scored lower, performed less well, and were more likely to drop out of school than children of older parents. The Council also found that children of teenage parents were more likely to exhibit behavioral problems in school.

The negative effects of poverty on academic performance and school retention are well documented. An analysis of the High School and Beyond study by Ruth Ekstrom and colleagues (1986) found socioeconomic status to be the strongest predictor of dropping out of school. While the national dropout rate is approximately 25 percent, rates among the economically disadvantaged are higher. As mentioned in Chapter 2, dropout rates in a number of America's largest cities are over 40 percent. Dropping out has a strong negative effect on an individual's future lifetime earnings and the chance to escape poverty. In a recent study, Michael Olneck (1989) estimated that a high school dropout will earn 16 to 28 percent less money over a lifetime than a high school graduate of similar cognitive ability and socioeconomic background. Olneck also estimated that remaining in school and graduating increases an individual's chances of escaping poverty by 50 percent.

An interesting implication of the study is that the employability and income of individuals in entry level jobs are less dependent on intelligence or performance than on simply graduating from high school. Regarding this point, Olneck (1989) observed

> I believe that as high school graduation becomes increasingly universal, characterizing the dropout as unqualified and irresponsible has become intensified. There is a social stigmatization of dropouts that exceeds their actual capabilities as employees. Public campaigns against dropping out of school contribute to branding of dropouts. . . . But at the same time you're persuading dropouts to stay in school, you're persuading others they're not worth hiring. (p. 11)

The economic displacements that have taken place the past fifteen to twenty years have resulted not only in the loss of financial capital among America's families but in the loss of social capital as well. According to James Coleman, social capital is "the range of exchange between parents and children about academic, social, economic, and personal matters" (1987, p. 37). With fewer adults in the home as a result of higher divorce rates and the increasing participation of mothers in the workforce, children have experienced an erosion of the social capital available to them.

Today more than 50 percent of mothers with school-age children work full time. One in two marriages ends in divorce. Thirty percent of all children have no adult at home when they return from school. While economic pressures are largely responsible for the absence of parents in children's lives, other factors have contributed as well. There has been an increasing desire for individualism and self-fulfillment among adults, manifested by concern over personal appearance, concentration upon career advancement, growth in conspicuous consumption, and decline in personal savings. An emphasis on one's own well-being is replacing a concern for others. Economic and personal fulfillment among adults are coming at the expense of America's children.

Writers such as Urie Bronfenbrenner (1977) and Neil Postman (1982) have observed these changes within our society. They note a reluctance among many adults to spend time with and take care of children. Unable or unwilling to take such responsibility, adults are increasingly turning to public and private institutions to meet the physical, emotional, and intellectual needs of the nation's children. While all children have been affected by the movement of adults out of the home and decreasing participation in childrearing, the trend has been most harmful to disadvantaged children. Advantaged parents are able to enroll their children in private schools and day care programs that provide the missing social capital of supervision and character formation on behalf of absent parents. Poor parents, on the other hand, do not have the economic resources to compensate for their increasing absence from the home. As a result, parents who cannot afford private options are increasingly asking government agencies such as schools to provide the missing social capital in their children's lives.

A 1989 survey commissioned by the Philip Morris Company and conducted by Louis Harris and Associates revealed the growing demand for child care. According to Harris, "People want action now. They're desperate for it. If there isn't action, I'll tell you—all hell will break loose" (quoted in Kalfus, 1989, p. 5-E). The survey found that while all American families with children under six years of age paid an average of $2,280 a year for child care, black American families paid $3,906. As Harris pointed out, "An old, old story in this country is that it costs more to be poor" (quoted in Kalfus, 1989, p. 5-E).

The poor have been joined by an increasing number of middle-class families, who find that not only is day care expensive, but the quality is unsatisfactory. Together, these parents are now pressuring public schools to provide extended day care in addition to educating their children during the regular school day. In response, an increasing number of school districts have begun offering before- and after-school latchkey programs. Some states, such as New York, are now considering public schooling for 3- and 4-year-olds so that working and single parents can be spared the expense of extended private day care.

In addition to an expansion in hours and age groups served, public schools are making changes in the content of the curriculum. Services to students have expanded dramatically in recent years in an attempt to meet a variety of social-psychological needs. Parental unwillingness and inability to assume responsibility for health care activities such as dental, eye, ear, and scoliosis checkups have forced schools to provide them. Schools likewise offer meals, sex education, career education, values clarification, counseling, and drug and alcohol rehabilitation. Curricula have been developed and implemented to reduce child and substance abuse, teenage pregnancies, AIDS, and juvenile crime.

As the public school takes on the role of social service agency as well as educational institution, the variety and quality of the social-psychological services provided will be among the measures by which some parents and community members evaluate their schools. Educational excellence will no longer be defined simply in terms of intellectual rigor or academic comprehensiveness but in terms of meeting a variety of economic, social, and psychological needs. The failure of schools to meet those needs can result in a loss of parental and community support.

The challenge facing public education in the 1990s and beyond is how to meet the varied demands and rising expectations for excellence in the social service sector and still deliver the traditional academic curriculum. It is questionable whether schools, as presently constructed, can successfully deliver everything expected of them. New educational institutions may be necessary to compensate for the missing social capital in children's lives. According to Coleman:

> The general shape of the demand for a new institution is clear: It is a demand not for further classroom indoctrination, nor for any particular content, but a demand for child care: *all day; from birth to school age; after school, every day, till parents return home from work; and all summer.* (1987, p. 38; emphasis in original)

Some school districts have begun to move in this direction. The Pomona, California, unified school district offers child care from morning to midnight. The district operates fifteen centers which provide all-day, year-round care for infants 6 weeks and older, preschoolers, and school-age children. The Independence, Missouri, school district provides before and after school child care for kindergartners to sixth-graders in ten of its thirteen elementary schools. It also operates two sites serving 3- and 4-year-olds. The Leadville, Colorado, school district has a child care program for 2½- to 13-year-olds. According to Wellesley College's Center for Research on Women, a survey of seven states revealed that approximately 17 percent of school districts were involved in some form of extended child care (Cohen, 1989a).

While some school districts have begun to serve preschool children and offer extended day care, they have typically done so on a self-supporting basis separate from the regular school program. At public alternative schools, especially those serving at-risk students, the provision of day care has traditionally been an integral part of the total program. Day care facilities at these schools usually serve students who have children. The facilities also serve as classrooms for instruction in parenting skills and child study. In addition to day care, many alternative schools and programs offer a variety of social-psychological services, such as counseling, drug and alcohol rehabilitation, work and independent study credits, and flexible scheduling, to their student clientele.

While comprehensive in the services they provide, few if any alternative schools offer their services as an integrated package inclusive of all age groups over an extended school year. Most public options, like their conventional counterparts, are designed to serve age-specific groups, such as preschool, primary, intermediate, or high school students, within the traditional 180-day school year. However, with the increasing demand for year-round child care for preschool as well as school-age children, school districts will be asked to reconsider the traditional calendar and age configurations they currently operate under. New models will be proposed to address the changing character of American family life. What might these new models look like? To find out, let's visit one model for the future already in operation.

A SCHOOL FOR THE TWENTY-FIRST CENTURY

Bethel school district serves several small bedroom communities just southeast of Tacoma, Washington. It is the second fastest growing school district in the state, with a current K–12 enrollment of 10,849 that is projected to increase to 14,290 by 1993. Bethel's students come primarily from middle- and lower-middle-class homes. Thirty-two percent of the children participate in the federal government's free or reduced-price lunch program. The minority enrollment is 17 percent. The district dropout rate is 23.8 percent, compared to a statewide average of 25 percent.

In 1974 Bethel established an alternative high school for at-risk students, and in 1984 it opened an alternative junior high school at a separate location. In 1987–88, the alternative high school enrolled approximately 175 students in grades 10–12, 56 of whom were teenage parents. The junior high school enrolled 35 students in grades 7–9. In addition to teenage parents, the two schools served students who had difficulty competing academically with their peers, fitting into one of the various social cliques at the conventional schools, or overcoming the inflexibility of traditional classroom instruction (10 percent of the alternative students have been identified as gifted). Problems related to substance abuse constituted another major factor in students' inability to function effectively in school. Many chose the alternative schools to get away from peer pressures that encouraged substance abuse. As with the Yakima alternative program, Bethel students had chosen to participate in the alternative schools; the district may not require individuals to attend.

Growing enrollment in Bethel's alternative junior and senior high schools prompted district administrators to examine the causes of student dissatisfaction with the conventional school program. In 1986 the district began surveying student attitudes about school. A questionnaire was administered to students in all three junior high schools and selected elementary schools. Responses indicated that some students had felt alienated from school as early as the primary grades. Results of the survey generated discussion among district administrators and teachers about possible changes in the secondary alternative program and the creation of an alternative program for at-risk elementary students.

In 1987, Governor Booth Gardner proposed and the Washington State Legislature enacted a $2.4 million program entitled, "Schools of the Twenty-first Century." The legislation provided funding for twenty-one innovative projects that could be models for schools of the future. Each project would receive $50,000 for each of six years, as well as funding to permit ten days of extended contracts for staff inservice. Last, and perhaps most important, projects would be allowed waivers from state regulations to facilitate implementation efforts. One hundred and thirty-five proposals were submitted to a selection committee, and the state board of education announced the winners in June 1988. Bethel school district's proposal for an "Extended Learning Family: A School from Birth to Adulthood" was among the twenty-one proposals chosen, the only alternative program to be selected. The proposal envisioned a centrally located, fully integrated alternative school to serve primarily at-risk individuals from preschool to young adulthood.

The first step was to find a single location so that all the alternative programs could be housed together. The District purchased ten acres in downtown Spanaway and built eleven small modules on the site. The cost of the land, buildings, and labor was approximately

$500,000. This expense, for a school of 300 students, represented less than one-twentieth of what the district had just spent to remodel the 900-student high school, providing further evidence that alternative education can be a cost-effective undertaking.

The second step was to change the traditional school day and calendar. The school year was lengthened from nine to eleven months to provide students with services over an extended period of time. The "Schools of the Twenty-first Century" grant had provided funding for ten additional inservice days, and the Bethel school district contributed money for nine more days, making it possible to operate school from the beginning of September to the end of July. Teacher pay was increased by 10 percent to compensate for the increased contract time. Teachers who did not wish to work the extra month did not have to. One teacher elected not to take advantage of the extended assignment, and another district teacher was hired in his place for the month of July. A four-day week was the next change to be introduced. Students would attend school Monday through Thursday. Fridays were to be set aside primarily for staff development, teacher inservice, program evaluation, conferences, and travel. Fridays were also to be used for special student projects, community work, fieldtrips, mentorships, and volunteer work.

The fall of 1988 saw the opening of Bethel's alternative junior and senior high programs, renamed "Voyager" and "Challenger" respectively, at their new site. The existing day care for children of teenage parents was expanded in size and services and renamed "Discovery Preschool." Three of the four components were in place by the beginning of the 1988–89 school year. The remainder of the year was spent integrating those three parts and planning for the addition of the elementary program in the fall of 1989.

Three groups of approximately sixty students are cycled four days a week through the Challenger program. The first group arrives at 8:00 A.M. and departs at 9:30 A.M. The second comes at 10:00 A.M. and leaves at 11:30 A.M. The last group attends from 12:30 to 2:00 P.M. The hour and a half at school is spent in a "family" of twelve students and one teacher. Here students work on basic skills, interpersonal relationships, and self-esteem. Four teacher/counselors help students develop self-confidence and concentrate on goal setting.

Academic credit is earned through contracted work done independently outside school. Students sign up for six courses (credits) of ninety hours each, which they complete at their own rate. Student progress is monitored and evaluated weekly by the "family" teacher/counselor. Teenage parents are placed in special "families" that meet for four hours. In addition to regular activities, teen parents receive instruction in parenting skills, hygiene, and nutrition. They also must assist in the preschool.

High school students wishing to enroll in Challenger must enter a transition class for four to six weeks. A transition teacher works with the students, assessing academic needs and reviewing needed basic skills. As in Challenger, the class meets Monday to Thursday for an hour and a half. Motivated students are able to earn one credit after four weeks. Students who demonstrate satisfactory attendance and academic progress may enter the Challenger program.

Voyager enrolls thirty-six students and occupies two modules, one for grades 7–8 and the other for grade 9. Twelve seventh- and eighth graders spend all day, four days a week, from 7:30 A.M. to 2:00 P.M., in a self-contained classroom with one teacher. These students have had difficulty adjusting to a variety of teachers and a curriculum divided into separate disciplines. Spending all day with one teacher is more reassuring to Voyager students, and the low student-teacher ratio allows for greater personal attention to individual needs. Since many students lack self-discipline and need structure, instruction is mostly whole-class and teacher-directed. Cooperative learning is used in teacher-assigned, small-group work. Independent study and contracted work are not used with seventh- and eighth-graders.

Ninth-grade students are located next door with another teacher. Two separate groups come for two-and-one-half-hour shifts that run from 7:30 to 10:00 A.M. and from 11:00 to 1:30 P.M., four days a week. Instruction is a combination of whole-class, small-group, and individualized study. In Voyager, an attempt is made to integrate the curriculum so that students see the interrelationships of various subjects, rather than learning each in isolation from one another.

The third component of the Extended Learning Family is Discovery Preschool. Discovery Preschool is new and grew out of the previous daycare program attached to the alternative high school. As part of the "Schools of the Twenty-first Century" grant, the district proposed to move beyond daycare by offering a formal preschool educational program to children eighteen to thirty-six months old. A certified preschool teacher was hired beginning in the fall of 1989. At present, the teacher and two instructional aides staff the two facilities, which operate from 8:00 A.M. to 4:00 P.M.

Discovery Preschool offers a host of services to children and their mothers. Two social workers provide daily individual counseling, support groups, and workshops in assertiveness training and countering physical and sexual abuse. The workers also serve as liaisons to drug and alcohol rehabilitative services, prenatal care, and Lamaze classes. The county health department provides a nurse who instructs teenage parents in the health care of their children. Child Reach provides twice yearly vision, hearing, motor, and language screening of the children. A Washington State University extension agent offers regular classes in nutrition. The daycare and preschool are well furnished. Each has an observation room with a one-way mirror to allow mothers to observe the social interaction of their children.

The Extended Learning Family incorporates advanced technology in its curriculum and instruction. Monies from the "Schools of the Twenty-first Century" grant have been used to purchase several high-technology teaching aids. Two laser disk players and a CD-ROM have been added to give students access to a variety of reference and instructional materials. Laser disks of Colliers Encyclopedia and the collection of the National Gallery of Art, as well as several history and science disks, have been purchased. The CD-ROM is a mass storage device that allows students to access large databases, generate personalized maps, and retrieve resource information. Students are able to conduct research on a variety of topics, copy segments onto videocassettes, and create both written reports and multimedia projects.

Fourteen Apple IIEs and a Macintosh SE are located in the technology center. These computers are used to facilitate the independent contract work students undertake. Hypercard stacks are being created for each of the learning contracts, and students will be able to preview courses along with teachers before selecting those most suitable for their academic needs. Each stack will contain performance objectives, a course outline, and evaluation criteria. A trained technician will supervise the lab and instruct students in word processing, database, spreadsheet, and telecommunications techniques.

The Extended Learning Family is currently negotiating with the Copen Foundation of New York. The plan is to provide face-to-face contact with pairs of children from different schools throughout the world to promote understanding through joint student projects. A satellite downlink at the technology lab is scheduled to be installed during the 1990–91 school year. This will allow students to participate in a variety of distance learning opportunities and supplement their individual learning contracts.

Teachers have been encouraged to familiarize themselves with the new technology. A district-funded Individual Instructional Improvement Projects (IIIP) grant provides all alternative teachers with $1,000 to $1,200 a year to enhance professional development. The money may be spent at the teacher's discretion. To date, four of the staff have purchased Macintoshes with the IIIP funds, while others have taken advanced coursework in instructional technology.

The fourth component of the Extended Learning Family, the Explorer Elementary Program, opened its doors in the fall of 1989. The program serves thirty children, grades 1–6, and is housed in two modules and staffed by two teachers and an instructional aide. Explorer features student-selected, self-paced learning experiences. The curriculum is interdisciplinary and utilizes the project method. Classroom learning centers incorporate a variety of themes or topics students may explore with teacher direction. The community is the major focus of the curriculum. Students make use of the town library, take frequent fieldtrips, and are assisted in class by community resource persons.

Parental involvement is an important component of Explorer. Since it is a school of choice, parent input in and support for curricular and instructional decisions is expected. Parents are encouraged to assist in daily instruction, serve as resource experts on a variety of theme-related topics and are required to participate ten hours a month if their children are to remain in the program.

Rather than letter grades children receive written teacher evaluations. Progress conferences are scheduled every forty-five days. The purpose of the conferences is to review individual learning plans and evaluate progress. Students progress at their own rate and may take more or less time to complete the primary or intermediate requirements. Cross-age tutoring is built into the instructional design. Intermediate students assist primary students as well as work cooperatively with individuals within their own block.

When originally conceived, Explorer was designed to serve at-risk students. The program characteristics of individualization, community orientation, cross-age grouping, and continuous progress were intended to attract and increase the success of elementary students who were beginning to show signs of alienation from traditional school. An unforeseen development took place, however, when the announcement for the new program was circulated among district patrons in the spring of 1989. Sign-up for the program was on a first-come, first-served basis, and the first to sign up were not primarily the parents of at-risk students but parents of high-achieving children who were attracted by the innovative, nontraditional option being offered. As a result, when Explorer opened its door in the fall of 1989, 75 percent of its student body was academically able and/or highly motivated.

At first, district administrators and teachers were surprised by the turn of events, but they now see the development as a blessing in disguise. The Extended Learning Family will now enroll both at-risk and regular students, eliminating the traditional segregation of the two groups. Most at-risk programs segregate students from their conventional counterparts, which can amplify negative behaviors because the at-risk students reinforce one another and their actions. By integrating both groups in a mutually satisfactory environment, the district hopes that negative behaviors will be reduced.

The sign-up and participation by parents of academically able and motivated students have given increased support and legitimacy to alternative education and the concept of choice. District patrons no longer see alternative schools and programs as options solely for at-risk or disadvantaged students. The opening of Explorer has generated a demand for additional schools and programs of choice. Bethel has begun planning a second elementary option similar to Explorer, to be opened during the 1990–91 school year, followed by a third in 1992–93. With these options care will be taken to insure increased participation by parents of at-risk children.

Expansion and extension of the Extended Learning Family was also planned for the next two years. Beginning in the winter of 1990, a community college introductory English class was offered at night. The class is designed for Challenger students, district classified staff, and community persons who might want to experience a college class and, perhaps, apply it toward a degree at the local community college. Challenger students may also count the course toward their high school graduation requirements. Additional introductory courses in sociology, history, psychology, computer literacy, and substance abuse are scheduled for the 1989–90 school year. In the fall of 1990, Challenger will begin offering a late afternoon "family" block, and in 1991 a Saturday morning "family" block for students who work full time. The eventual plan is to offer a number of programs that serve preschool children to young adults and to operate morning to evening eleven months out of the year.

Will the Extended Learning Family really become a school that serves the community from birth to adulthood? It is too early to tell, but if student and parent interest are any indication, the outlook is bright. Currently, there are waiting lists for all four programs. At the start of its second year of operation (1989–90), ten teenage parents were waiting to get their children into the day care or preschool. Fifty students were on Challenger's waiting list, and eight on Voyagers. Forty-six parents, including one pregnant mother, have placed their children's names on the waiting list for Explorer.

Bethel's attempt to increase parental participation and choice, expand student services over an extended school year, and introduce technology to facilitate teaching and learning are all steps toward creating an effective public school for the twenty-first century.

THE MOVEMENT TOWARD PRIVATIZATION

While an all-inclusive, expanded-care, year-round school is one model some embrace, it would be a mistake to see it as the only model public education should endorse. Many students neither need nor want the services offered at the Extended Learning Family. Parents who are able and willing to provide the necessary social capital for their children would find an expanded care, year-round school an unnecessary duplication of many services provided at home. Parents who are not enthusiastic supporters of public education would be reluctant to allow their children to attend school from birth to adulthood. One model, no matter how innovative or comprehensive, will never satisfy all students and their families.

Educational theorists, such as James Coleman in the 1960s and Phillip Cusick in the 1970s, have reminded us of this fact. Both have documented the difficulty conventional public schools, particularly the comprehensive high school, have had in trying to meet the needs of a diverse student body. As the Panel on Youth of the President's Science Advisory Committee (1974) concluded: "The problem is most acute when a single form, the public high school, attempts single-handedly to meet the increasing spread of group demands and cultural tasks. But a variety of needs can only be met by a variety of institutions" (p. 90).

More recent observations on the undesirability of a single model for schools and public education have come from a number of theorists. Michael Apple (1982), Henry Giroux (1983), and Peter McLaren (1989) have focused on the role public schools play in maintaining the moral and intellectual leadership of the dominant social and economic groups within our society. They claim that schools attempt to define meaning and assign a "common" worldview that all students are expected to accept. This is done through the process of hegemony and the content of the hidden curriculum. Some individuals and subgroups, however, resist the worldview offered by schools. Most notable among the resisters are racial and ethnic minorities and the economically disadvantaged. Whether one endorses this critique of public education or not, it does seem clear that the conventional public school, as presently constructed, is simply not working for large numbers of American children. It has managed to alienate both the economically disadvantaged, who drop out in large numbers, and the economically advantaged, who patronize nonpublic alternatives.

While much of the discussion in this chapter has focused on the disadvantaged, affluent and middle-income families are also expressing dissatisfaction with public education. Increasing numbers are leaving public schools and choosing private educational options. Why are they leaving? While much of the exodus can be attributed to white resistance to racial integration, that is not the sole reason. Growing dissatisfaction with the quality of public schools is also a major factor. In the words of one parent, "Public education too often means indifference, incompetence, nonaccountability, and faddism" (Petroski, 1984, p. 15). Some public schools have lost touch with the families they serve; they have failed to remain close to their customers.

The consolidation of school districts and the bureaucratization of public education have left parents further removed from their children's education. In addition, the movement toward greater state funding of public education, while necessary to insure equity, has lessened community control and the sense of local ownership of the schools. As we saw in Chapter 3, big schools do not always mean better schools. The same holds true for school bureaucracies. As Ferdinand Colloredo-Mansfeld of the Boston Private Industry Council has noted, "The problem with the school system is the highly centralized bureaucracy. That bureaucratic structure has lost sight of the mission—the children" (quoted in Walker, 1989, p. 5).

Changing school organization is the key to achieving academic excellence according to John Chubb (1989) of the Brookings Institution, who studied 500 public and private high schools around the country. Chubb found that "Neither expenditures, teacher salaries, class size, graduation requirements, the amount of homework assigned, or any other individual school policy that we looked at matters. . . . The thing about schools that really matters is how they are organized" (p. 6).

Chubb identified autonomy from external control as the key organizational factor. In successful schools, principals and teachers were given the independence and influence to experiment and make programmatic decisions, while their counterparts at unsuccessful schools were not. Teachers at successful schools were free to design practices and materials to meet the needs of their students, and they participated more in school decisions. Principals at successful schools had greater on-site authority over curriculum, instruction, hiring, firing, and discipline.

Private schools were more likely than public ones to be autonomous, in part because of their status but also because private schools needed to attract clients to survive. According to Chubb (1989), "One way that you do that and keep parents and students happy, is to ensure that decisions are made at the level of the individual school, which is where the parents and students confront the system" (p. 9).

Decisions in public education are rarely made at the level of the individual school. The legacy of nineteenth-century industrialization, with its emphasis on standardization and a "scientific" approach to curriculum and instruction, still characterizes the approach of most school districts. This legacy, combined with public education's status as a near monopoly, has discouraged schools from experimenting or seeking change on their own. As Gerald Zaltman and colleagues (1977) have observed: "Public educational institutions are in a unique position with regard to ignoring forces for change. They enjoy the 'protected status' of a public agency with a conscripted clientele and are less subject to the immediate pressure of the marketplace" (p. 30). This "protected status" can contribute to an unresponsive attitude when patrons ask for changes in the management of public education or in the services provided. Unlike private corporations, public schools do not have to secure customer satisfaction to stay in business. Most of their customers are guaranteed.

While most of the customers are guaranteed, many are not satisfied. Some families are making their educational selection from the variety of private schools available. Exercising this choice requires money, however. Middle- and upper-income American families find it easier to take advantage of private options, but an increasing number of minority and economically disadvantaged parents are also opting for a private education for their children. One of the most affordable options available to minority and poor families is the Catholic school system. Minority enrollment in America's elementary and secondary Catholic schools increased from 11 percent in 1971 to 22 percent in 1987. Non-Catholic enrollment, the majority of which was black, increased from 3 percent to 12 percent during the same time (Pavuk, 1987). The choice of private education represents a substantial sacrifice for poor and minority families. The fact that increasing numbers of them are making the sacrifice indicates a widespread dissatisfaction with traditional public education.

A growing dissatisfaction with public services in general has prompted some cities and towns to consider privatization as a possible answer to the problem of declining quality. Privatization involves contracting private operators to provide traditional public services, such as trash collection, law enforcement, job training, drug rehabilitation, even public education. Regarding privatization of public education, Marilyn Block, executive vice president of the John Naisbett Group, has observed: "You make a list of tasks to be done—raising reading, math, and Scholastic Aptitude Test scores, increasing the number of graduates going to college—and then look for a private sector business to supply the service" (quoted in "Getting a jump on the trailblazers," 1988–89, p. 50).

The trend toward privatization is a growing one that is predicted to continue and provide competition for a number of public agencies, including schools. The Milwaukee public schools have contracted with private schools since 1982 to provide alternative programs for at-risk middle and high school students. In 1988, it began contracting with daycare centers to offer kindergarten and child care to disadvantaged 4- and 5-year-olds. In 1989 the school board proposed extending privatization to 1,000 at-risk disadvantaged elementary students. These children would be able to attend district-approved private schools to receive their education. While the Wisconsin state legislature failed to approve the proposal, legislators will undoubtedly be asked to reconsider the proposal in the 1990s.

One of the most dramatic examples of the privatization of public education was the decision by Chelsea, Massachusetts, to place its entire school system in the hands of Boston University for a ten year period beginning in the fall of 1989. In consigning parts of the system to private contractors, as Milwaukee has done, or all of it, as Chelsea has done, both districts have admitted an inability to provide an effective public education program for all of their children.

In Chicago several major corporations did not wait for the city's school system to admit failure and decided to fund and operate their own private elementary school. In 1988, Sears Roebuck, United Airlines, Premark International, and Baxter International opened the Corporate/Community School in Lawndale, one of Chicago's poorest neighborhoods. One thousand children applied for 150 openings in grade K–3. Over the next few years the Corporate/Community School will be expanded to serve 300 children in grades K–8. The corporate executives who conceived and financed the school hope it will become a model the Chicago public schools can adopt. The experiments in Chicago, Chelsea, and Milwaukee illustrate a growing dissatisfaction with public education and a willingness to consider private alternatives.

THE CASE FOR OPTIONS AND CHOICE

If public education hopes to slow the movement toward privatization, it must provide alternatives that are competitive with those in the private sector. If public schools fail to offer a variety of attractive options from which students and their parents may choose, they will continue to lose not only the 25 to 40 percent of economically disadvantaged and underachieving students who drop out but also the economically advantaged and highly motivated students who are increasingly patronizing private education.

This realization has prompted a number of urban school districts, such as those of New York, Chicago, and Boston, to push for decentralization and the introduction of more community and parent involvement in setting educational policy. Greater autonomy for teachers and on-site administrators and parental choice in school selection have also been introduced. While no panacea, increased options and choice can be partial answers to the problem of declining quality in and dissatisfaction with public education. At the very least, they provide a much-needed prod to an increasingly bureaucratic and insensitive system.

Choices tailored to meet the needs of students and their families can provide both effectiveness and equity in our public schools. According to Charles Glenn, Director of the Massachusetts Education Department's Office of Educational Equity,

> Choice can do much to promote equity. It does so by creating conditions which encourage schools to become more effective . . . by allowing schools to specialize and thus to meet the needs of some students very well rather than all students at a level of minimum adequacy, and by increasing the influence of parents over the education of their children in a way which is largely conflict-free. (quoted in Nathan, 1989, p. 24)

The effectiveness of public schools of choice has been documented in numerous research studies. Mary Anne Raywid (1989) has found more than 100 studies indicating that when families are allowed to select among different district schools and programs, student achievement and attitudes improve. Examples of successful public schools and programs of choice that have gained national attention include ones in New York City, Cambridge, Massachusetts, and Prince George's County, Maryland.

East Harlem is among the poorest and most educationally disadvantaged areas of New York City. When its magnet program first started, East Harlem was ranked thirty-second in achievement among New York's thirty-two community school districts; in 1989 it was sixteenth. In 1978, only 15 percent of East Harlem's students scored at the national norm in reading levels; in 1989, 60 percent did. Cambridge has seen its student achievement test scores rise every year since introducing controlled choice in its elementary schools in 1982. In addition, the gap between black and white students' achievement has decreased. In 1980, Prince George's County had some of the worst schools in the Washington, D.C. area. In 1985, the district established forty-four magnet schools. In 1989, average scores on the California Achievement Test were 70 percent, a considerable improvement from the 50 percent in 1985.

While options and choice have been shown to be effective in improving education, critics caution that they may not be beneficial for everyone. Some see public schools of choice contributing to the traditional sorting function of American public education. They claim that options are often designed to segregate students into inferior and superior programs. This promotes elitism and further aggravates inequities within a school district. Options, with selection criteria for admission, siphon off the better students from conventional schools, leaving them without role models and further demoralizing teachers, administrators, and the students who remain behind. Higher per pupil expenditures of some options divert much needed financial resources from their conventional counterparts, compounding the problem of limited resources.

In their study of public alternative schools, Robert Arnove and Toby Strout (1978) concluded that options for at-risk students were used primarily to remove and isolate them from mainstream schools and programs. Undesirable students were "dumped" into remedial programs, which were disproportionately poor and minority in composition. In their study of four urban school districts, Donald Moore and Suzanne Davenport (1989) found that while students in magnet schools received excellent and more costly curricula and instruction, students who remained in neighborhood schools did not. They observed that many options had selection criteria for participation and attracted students with better than average test scores, grades, attendance, and behavior. As a result, the better students were siphoned off, leaving neighborhood schools with lower-achieving and less well behaved students. Moore and Davenport also found many options to have complex admission criteria, which required parental initiative and knowledge of the school system. They observed that

some families did not have the time or skill to master the intricacies necessary to have their children admitted to a special program or school.

In Chapter 1 we learned that the continuation school for at-risk students is the most popular option among public schools of choice. National and Washington state surveys indicated that approximately two-thirds of alternative students were performing below local achievement levels, and administrators associated alternative schools with "disruptive," "turned-off," or "disinterested" students (Raywid, 1982; Young, 1988). Chapter 5, on Yakima's alternative school and programs, confirmed that at-risk options serve a student clientele that is, if not minority, disproportionately poor.

The question is whether these students are being "dumped" into alternative schools and programs and segregated from traditional schools. "Dumped" implies that individuals are forced to attend remedial options. As we saw with the Yakima and Bethel alternative programs, this is not the case. Remedial as well as other options operate on the basis of choice. Students do not have to attend them. In fact, many students in at-risk programs are at or beyond the leaving age and may drop out whenever they wish. Unlike their conventional counterparts, public schools of choice attract their students on the basis of customer satisfaction.

Options for at-risk students represent an attempt by school districts to bring dissatisfied individuals back into the school system. Continuation schools, learning centers, and other options have been designed not to segregate certain groups of students but to return individuals who have rejected the comprehensive high school model of education. The success of these options has been dependent not on coercion but on successfully meeting students' needs.

While some public schools of choice do have admission requirements, most do not. Rolf Blank's 1984 study of forty-five magnet schools found 33 percent to have selection criteria such as attendance, test score, and grade-point average requirements. The many options for at-risk students do not have admission requirements. In fact, their student clientele is made up of individuals who have had difficulty meeting the selection criteria of traditional schools. Nor is it clear that the admission requirements of options are the main cause for the enrollment decline and demoralization of urban neighborhood schools. The problems of urban public education predate magnet schools and are the result of chronic and complex circumstances.

Eliminating options and choice will not raise morale or enrollment at neighborhood schools. It will only accelerate the movement of students to private education. Evidence for this conclusion is found in a survey of Boston parents by the Citywide Educational Coalition (1985). When private school parents were asked if they would return to public education if given the opportunity to select a "high quality" public school anywhere in the district, many said they would "very seriously" consider transferring back to the public system.

Magnet schools do cost from 10 to 12 percent more to operate than neighborhood schools, but the cost differential between the two declines the longer the magnet school is in operation. But while magnets may cost more, nonmagnet options cost less to operate than their conventional counterparts. Studies by Mary Anne Raywid (1982) and Gary Wehlage (1983) support this conclusion. As discussed in Chapter 2, school districts actually make money on most public schools of choice, especially those designed to serve at-risk students. As we saw in Bethel's establishment of its Extended Learning Family (earlier in this chapter), alternative schools and programs can be a cost-effective move for school districts to undertake.

Lack of knowledge about various options and the procedures for enrolling children in them has resulted in underparticipation by disadvantaged and minority families in schools and programs of choice. Moore and Davenport's (1989) concern is supported by Susan Uchitelle's (1978) study of a midwestern school district, which revealed that minority and low-income parents were not as knowledgeable about the opportunities for choice as their middle- and upper-income counterparts. The Rand study of Alum Rock's voucher experiment (A Study of Alternatives . . . , 1981) drew similar conclusions. Indeed, the enrollment for the Explorer elementary program in Bethel is further evidence of differences in parental knowledge and action.

While the concern about informed and equitable participation in options is a real one, it and other objections voiced by critics can be addressed satisfactorily and need not prevent school districts from introducing options and choice to their patrons. Joe Nathan (1988), a long time supporter of choice, suggests a number of preconditions to introducing options within a school district.

- Free transportation to facilitate participation by all families
- Implementation of racial-balance procedures to prevent segregation
- A wide range of programs at many schools rather than a limited number of programs at a few selected schools

- Provision of information and counseling to facilitate parental selection
- Avoidance of selective criteria for participation in options

Nathan's preconditions go a long way in answering the objections of critics. Provision of information and counseling regarding available options, as well as free transportation, insure greater participation by all families interested in choice. The elimination of selective criteria and the implementation of racial and socioeconomic balance procedures prevent options from becoming elitist and siphoning off the better students.

One approach to preventing racial and socioeconomic imbalance among options within a school district is controlled choice. Parents indicate their first through third preferences for schools, and the district attempts to accommodate those preferences while insuring that ethnic and economic imbalances do not result. Controlled choice represents a compromise between complete freedom to choose one's own school and compulsory district assignment of schools. Controlled choice will not satisfy everyone, especially those families that do not get their first choice, but it does provide some institutional flexibility and sense of personal control while maintaining the ideal of pluralism and integration in public education. Boston and Seattle are two urban school districts that have recently undertaken the controlled choice approach.

A wide range of choices rather than a limited number of options insures greater participation in and support for public schools. More options facilitate a more equitable distribution of education monies throughout a district, since financing is not concentrated on a few special programs or schools. The ideal solution is to make all of the schools in a district options, as Montclair, New Jersey, and Richmond, California have done. To be successful, each option must be perceived by the community as being of similar quality. If some are seen as inferior in the resources they receive or in the students they serve, community support will be undermined. This does not mean, however, that all options must be identical. A misconception among some educational theorists and practitioners is that equality means sameness and that any difference is bad and must be avoided. As Gerald Grant (1988) reminds us, such reasoning is faulty:

> The laudable effort to overcome harmful inequalities has led to the presumption that all difference between schools must be extinguished on the grounds that they reflect inequalities. . . .

Tolstoy was wrong when he wrote that "all happy families are like one another. They are alike in that they are happy, but the kinds and qualities of happiness and the forms and activities through which it is achieved are many. If each slavishly followed a plan for happy families developed by the ministry, they might be more alike but fewer would be happy. So it is with schools. (p. 222)

Grant's observation is confirmed by the six alternative schools and programs described in Chapter 4. While all are exemplary, each is different in the program offered and the student clientele served. Good schools, like good teachers, need not be alike. It is time to recognize that, just as consumers are best served by a variety of quality stores, so students are best served by a variety of quality schools. The key word here is *quality*. Choice, by itself, will not make schools better. A variety of poor schools is no improvement over a single poor school. Funding at adequate levels and a commitment to public education must continue if alternative schools and programs are to bring change and improvement to teaching and learning. Support for alternative education is not an excuse to cut schools loose and let them fend for themselves. Nor is it a stalking horse for the introduction of educational vouchers that would transfer financial support from public to private schools.

Public alternative education is not a disguise to allow individuals to resegregate on the basis of racial, social, or economic backgrounds. Public schools of choice may not exclude students who might present an extra financial or instructional burden; neither may they operate under an educational philosophy that has as its main purpose the exclusion of "undesirable" students. Students and their families choose options. Alternative schools and programs do not choose students.

If choice and options are to lead to school improvement, they must be combined with organizational changes such as those proposed in the 1989 Carnegie Report, *Turning Points: Preparing American Youth for the 21st Century*. The seventeen-member Task Force on Education of Young Adolescents recommended: "Dividing large, impersonal schools into smaller 'communities for learning,' where stable, close, and mutually respectful relationships with adults and peers can be forged . . . and empowering both teachers and administrators by giving them greater voices in decisionmaking and governance" (quoted in Rothman, 1989, p. 21). The task force called for the creation of school within a school and "house" arrangements to personalize the school experience, noting that "young adolescents have a great need for intimacy, yet we put them in large impersonal schools,. . . .

Young adolescents need increased autonomy and they need to make their own decisions" (quoted in Rothman, 1989, p. 21). Additional recommendations made by the task force included the elimination of ability grouping, the introduction of the cooperative learning and cross-age tutoring approaches, and the provision of increased health and social services.

These recommendations embrace the characteristics found in effective public schools of choice. Smallness, concern for the whole student, supportive environment, and sense of community/clear mission hold the key not only for successful alternative schools and programs but for all schools. These characteristics provide hope not only for the present but, as the Carnegie Report reminds us, for preparing American youth for the twenty-first century.

The time for change is now. The twenty-first century is almost upon us. If we fail to increase options and choice within public education, the exodus from public schools will not only continue but will accelerate. America will become a society even more divided into educational haves who choose private schools and educational have-nots who must attend public schools. The result would be further decline into educational mediocrity.

Will the introduction of choice and options solve all the problems of a divided America? Is public alternative education *the* solution to America's declining educational fortunes? Some years ago, Lawrence Cremin (1978) paraphrased a wise nineteenth-century social reformer, saying, "using education to correct social injustice was about as effective as using rosewater to cure the plague" (p. 206). Public alternative education is not El Dorado. More choice and a variety of better schools will not eliminate poverty, illiteracy, teenage drug use, or crime. The causes of these problems involve long-standing and complex political, social, and economic factors. Solutions to these problems must be found outside public education in the political and economic institutions of our society.

What public alternative education can do is initiate the problem solving process by calling attention to inequities within our society. Public alternative schools and programs can improve student performance by placing less emphasis on individual competition and a narrow definition of school success. Options and choice can increase school effectiveness by empowering administrators, teachers, parents, and students and by creating more humane and autonomous environments. Together, these reforms offer partial solutions to achieving educational excellence and equity in our schools and correcting social injustice in our society.

References

Apple, M. W. (1982). *Education and power.* Boston: Routledge & Kegan Paul.

Arnove, R., & Strout, T. (1978). Alternative schools: Cultural pluralism and reality. *Educational Research Quarterly, 2*(4), 75–95.

Barbanel, J. (1988, April 12). How despair is engulfing a generation of New York. *New York Times,* p. E6.

Barker, R. G., & Gump, P. V. (1964). *Big school, small school.* Stanford, CA: Stanford University Press.

Barr, R. D. (1975). The growth of alternative public schools: The 1975 ICOPE report. *Changing Schools, 12,* 9.

Blank, R. K. (1984). The effects of magnet schools on the quality of education in urban school districts. *Phi Delta Kappan, 66*(4), 270–272.

Boyer, E. L. (1983). *High school: A report on secondary education in America.* New York: Harper & Row.

Bronfenbrenner, U. (1977). The disturbing changes in the American family. *Education Digest, 42*(6), 22–25.

Brown, F. B. (1963). *The nongraded high school.* Englewood Cliffs, NJ: Prentice-Hall.

Carnegie Council on Adolescent Development. (1989). Turning points: Preparing American youth for the 21st century. Washington, DC: Carnegie Council.

Chubb, J. (1989). Making schools better: Choice and educational improvement. *Equity and Choice, 5*(3), 5–10.

Citywide Educational Coalition. (1985). *A study of attitudes among parents of elementary school children in Boston.* Boston: Martilla & Kiley Associates.

CLASS Newsletter (1989, March). Educational Service District 105. 7(6).

Cohen, D. L. (1989a, April 19). Growing number of schools are filling demand for child care. *Education Week,* pp. 1, 20.

Cohen, D. L. (1989b, May 17). Milwaukee proposal on private schools stirs debate. *Education Week,* p. 7.

Coleman, J. S. (1961). *The adolescent society.* New York: Free Press.

Coleman, J. S. (1981). Quality and equality in American education: Public and Catholic schools. *Phi Delta Kappan, 63*(3), 159–164.

Coleman, J. S. (1987). Families and schools. *Educational Researchers, 16*(7), 32–38.

127

Comer, J. P. (1985). Demand for excellence and the need for equity. In Fantini, M. and Sinclair, R. (Eds.), *Education in school and nonschool settings* (pp. 245–263). Chicago: University of Chicago Press.

Coons, J. E., & Sugarman, S. D. (1978). *Education by choice.* Berkeley: University of California Press.

Cremin, L. A. (1978). The free school movement: A perspective. In T. E. Deal & R. R. Nolan (Eds.), *Alternative schools* (pp. 203–210). Chicago: Nelson-Hall.

Curriculum planning and evaluation. (1987). *An impact evaluation on the environmental education program.* Grand Rapids, MI: Grand Rapids Public Schools.

Cusick, P. A. (1973). *Inside high school: The student's world.* New York: Holt, Rinehart & Winston.

Digest of educational statistics. (1988). Washington, DC: National Center for Educational Statistics.

Doremus, R. R. (1981). Whatever happened to . . . John Adams high school? *Phi Delta Kappan, 63*(3), 199–202.

Doremus, R. R. (1982). Whatever happened to . . . Melbourne high school? *Phi Delta Kappan, 63*(7), 480–482.

Doyle, D. P., & Levine, M. (1984). Magnet schools: Choice and quality in public education. *Phi Delta Kappan, 66*(4), 265–270.

Duke, D. L., & Muzio, I. (1978). How effective are alternative schools? A review of recent evaluations and reports. *Teachers College Record, 79*(3), 461–483.

Education almanac. (1984). Reston, VA: National Association of Elementary School Principals.

Education Commission of the States. Law and Education Center. (1986). *Footnotes.* No. 22. Denver, CO: Author.

Ehrenreich, B. (1986, September 7). Is the middle class doomed? *New York Times Magazine,* p. 44.

Ekstrom, R. B., Goertz, M., Pollack, J. M., & Rock, D. (1986). Who drops out of high school and why? Findings from a national study. *Teachers College Record, 87*(3), 356–373.

Erickson, D. A. (1982). *The British Columbia story: Antecedents and consequences of aid to private schools.* Los Angeles, CA: Institute for the Study of Private Schools.

Facts about Yakima, Washington and the Yakima valley. (1989). Yakima: Greater Yakima Chamber of Commerce.

Featherstone, J. (1967a). How children learn. *The New Republic, 157*(10), 17–21.

Featherstone, J. (1967b). Schools for children. *The New Republic, 157*(8&9), 17–21.

Featherstone, J. (1967c). Teaching children to think. *The New Republic, 157*(11), 15–19.

Fleming, P. S., Blank, R. K., Dentler, R. A., & Baltzell, D. C. (1982). *Survey of magnet schools: Interim report for the U.S. Department of Education.* Washington, DC: James H. Lowry and Associates.

Foley, E., & Crull, P. (1984). *Educating the at-risk student. More lessons from alternative high schools.* New York: Public Education Association.

Foley, E. M., & McConnaughy, S. B. (1982). *Towards school improvement: Lessons from alternative high schools.* New York: Public Education Association.

Friedenberg, E. Z. (1959). *The vanishing adolescent.* New York: Dell.

Friedman, M. (1962). *Capitalism and freedom.* Chicago: University of Chicago Press.

Gallup, A. M., & Clark, D. L. (1987). The 19th annual Gallup poll of the public's attitudes towards the public schools. *Phi Delta Kappan, 69* (1), 17–30.

Garbarino, J. (1980). Some thoughts on school size and its effects on adolescent development. *Journal of Youth and Adolescents, 9*(1), 19–31.

Getting a jump on the trailblazers. (1988–89, December 26–January 2). *Insight,* p. 50.

Gibbons, M. (1974). Walkabout: Searching for the right passage from childhood and school. *Phi Delta Kappan, 55*(9), 596–602.

Ginott, H. (1973). Driving children sane. *Today's Education, 63*(7), 20–25.

Giroux, H. (1983). *Theory and resistance: A pedagogy for the opposition.* South Hadley, MA: Bergin and Garvey.

Glasser, W. (1986). *Control theory in the classroom.* New York: Harper & Row.

Gold, M., & Mann, D. W. (1984). *Expelled to a friendlier place: A study of effective alternative schools.* Ann Arbor: University of Michigan Press.

Goodlad, J. I. (1984). *A place called school.* New York: McGraw-Hill.

Goodlad, J. I., et al. (1975). *The conventional and the alternative in education.* Berkeley, CA: McCutchan.

Goodman, P. (1964a). *Compulsory mis-education and the community of scholars.* New York: Vintage.

Goodman, P. (1964b). *Growing up absurd.* New York: Random House.

Grabe, M. (1976). Big school, small school: Impact of the high school environment. *Contemporary Educational Psychology, 1,* 20–25.

Grant, G. (1988). *The world we created at Hamilton high.* Cambridge, MA: Harvard University Press.

Graubard, A. (1972). *Free the children: Radical reform and the free school movement.* New York: Pantheon.

Gregory, T. B., & Smith, G. R. (1987). *High schools as communities: Small schools reconsidered.* Bloomington, IN: Phi Delta Kappa.

Haberman, M. (1988). *Preparing teachers for urban schools.* Bloomington, IN: Phi Delta Kappa.

Hahn, A. (1987). Reaching out to America's dropouts: What to do. *Phi Delta Kappan, 69*(4), 256–263.

Hentoff, N. (1967). *Our children are dying.* New York: Viking.

Hill, J. (1987). *Learning unlimited 1985–86 a follow-up report.* Indianapolis, IN: Metropolitan School District of Washington Township.

Holt, J. C. (1964). *How children fail.* New York: Delta.

Holt, J. C. (1967). *How children learn.* New York: Dell.

Ianni, F. A., & Reuss-Ianni, E. (1979). School crime and the social order of the school. *IRCD Bulletin, 14*(1), 2–11.

Illich, I. (1971). *Deschooling society.* New York: Harper & Row.

Jencks, C. (1970). Education vouchers: A report on financing elementary education by grants to parents. Cambridge: Center for the Study of Public Policy.

Johnson, D. W., & Johnson, R. T. (1987). *Learning together and alone.* Englewood Cliffs, NJ: Prentice-Hall.

Jones, J. D. (1988). The six school complex. *Equity and Choice IV*(2), 31–38.

Kalfus, M. (1989, April 16). Majority believes youngsters have it worse today than ever before. *Yakima Herald Republic,* p. 5-E.

Kammann, R. (1972). The case for making each school in your district "different." *American School Board Journal, 159*(7), 37, 38.

Kellogg, J. B. (1988). Forces of change. *Phi Delta Kappan, 70*(3), 199–204.

Kohl, H. R. (1967). *36 children.* New York: Signet.

Kozol, J. (1967). *Death at an early age.* New York: Bantam.

Kunisawa, B. (1988). A nation in crisis: The dropout dilemma. *NEA Today, 6*(6), 61–65.

Levin, H., & Thomas, J. (Eds.) (1983). *Public dollars for private schools: The case of tuition tax credits.* Philadelphia: Temple University Press.

Lindsay, P. (1982). The effect of high school size on student participation, satisfaction and attendance. *Educational Evaluation and Policy Analysis, 4*(1), 57–65.

Lindsay, P. (1984). High school size, participation in activities, and young adult social participation: Some enduring effects of schooling. *Educational Evaluation and Policy Analysis, 6*(1), 73–83.

London, P. (1987). Character education and clinical intervention: A paradigm shift for U.S. schools. *Phi Delta Kappan, 68*(9), 667–669.

Maslow, A. H. (1970). *Motivation and personality.* New York: Harper & Row.

McClellan, M. C. (1987). Teenage pregnancy. *Phi Delta Kappan, 68*(10), 789–792.

McCluskey, N. G. (1969). *Catholic education faces the future.* Garden City: Doubleday.

McLaren, P. (1989). *Life in schools.* New York: Longman.

Metz, M. H. (1986). *Different by design. The context and character of three magnet schools.* New York: Routledge & Kegan Paul.

Middle class squeeze. (1986, August 18). *U.S. News & World Report,* pp. 36–41.

Miller, S. E., Leinhardt, G., & Zigmond, N. (1988). Influencing engagement through accommodation: An ethnographic study of at-risk students. *American Educational Research Journal, 25*(4), 465–487.

Moore, D. R., & Davenport, S. (1989). High school choice and students at risk. *Equity and Choice, 5*(1), 5–10.

Mortimore, P., Sammons, P., Stoll, L., Lewis, D., & Ecob, R. (1988). *School matters.* Berkeley: University of California Press.

Nathan, J. (1988). Who benefits from options in urban education? *National Center on Effective Schools Newsletter, 3*(2), 9–11.

Nathan, J. (1989, April 19). Interdistrict programs offer 'expanded' opportunities. *Education Week*, pp. 24, 32.

National Coalition of Advocates for Children. (1985). *Barriers to excellence: Our children at risk.* Boston: Author.

National Commission on Excellence in Education. (1983). *A nation at risk.* Washington, DC: U.S. Government Printing Office.

National Governors' Association. (1986). *Time for results: The governors' 1991 report on education.* Washington, DC: Center for Policy Research and Analysis.

National Panel on High School and Adolescent Education. (1976). *The education of adolescents: The final report and recommendations.* Washington, DC: U.S. Government Printing Office.

National Research Council. (1987). *Risking the future: Adolescent sexuality, pregnancy, and childbearing.* Washington, DC: National Academy Press.

Neill, A. S. (1960). *Summerhill.* New York: Hart.

Nelson, G. E. (1989, January 7). Davis dropout rate 54%? *Yakima Herald Republic.* 1A, 7A.

New York State Education Department. (1985). *New York state magnet school research study.* MAGI Educational Services.

Olneck, M. R. (1989). Dropping out: Does it make a difference? *National Center on Effective Secondary Schools Newsletter, 4*(1), 10, 11.

Olsen, L., & Moore, M. (1982). *Voices from the classroom: Students and teachers speak out on the quality of teaching in our schools.* Oakland, CA: Citizens Policy Center.

Panel on Youth of the President's Science Advisory Committee. (1974). *Youth: Transition to adulthood.* Chicago: University of Chicago Press.

Pavuk, A. (1987, April 22). Catholic schools continue slide in enrollment. *Education Week*, p. 9.

Perhaps the single most promising reform idea. (1989, January 18). *Education Week*, p. 24.

Perkinson, H. J. (1976). *Two hundred years of American educational thought.* New York: Longman.

Peters, T. J., & Waterman, R. H., Jr. (1983). *In search of excellence.* New York: Warner Books.

Petroski, C. (1984, February 10). Why we chose private schools. *Christian Science Monitor*, p. 15.

The Portland Investment: A regional plan to combat youth unemployment. (1987). Portland, OR: The Leaders Roundtable.

Postman, N. (1982). *The disappearance of childhood.* New York: Delacorte.

Postman, N., & Weingartner, C. (1971a). *The soft revolution.* New York: Delacorte.

Postman, N., & Weingartner, C. (1971b). *Teaching us a subversive activity.* New York: Delacorte.

Postman, N., & Weingartner, C. (1973). *The school book.* New York: Delta.

Powell, A., Farrar, E., & Cohen, D. K. (1985). *The shopping mall high school.* Boston: Houghton Mifflin.

Putka, G. (1989, March 31). A matter of choice: Letting parents choose schools raises enthusiasm and controversy. *Wall Street Journal,* pp. R-16–17.

Raywid, M. A. (1981). The first decade of public school alternatives. *Phi Delta Kappan, 62*(8), 551–557.

Raywid, M. A. (1982). *The current status of schools of choice.* Hempstead, NY: Project on Alternatives in Education.

Raywid, M. A. (1989). *The case for public schools of choice.* Bloomington, IN: Phi Delta Kappa.

Research and Policy Committee. (1985). *Investing in our children.* New York: Committee for Economic Development.

Riessman, F. (1962). *The culturally deprived child.* New York: Harper & Row.

Rothman, R. (1989, June 21). Middle grades called "powerful" shaper of adolescents. *Education Week,* pp. 1, 21.

Schneider, J. (1986). Higher standards may boost number of dropouts. *Equity and Choice, 3*(1), 14, 15.

Slavin, R. E. (1983). *Cooperative learning.* New York: Longman.

Smith, G. R., Gregory, T. B., & Pugh, R. C. (1981). Meeting student needs: Evidence for the superiority of alternative schools. *Phi Delta Kappan, 62*(8), 561–564.

Smith, V. H. (1974). *Alternative schools: The development of options in public education.* Lincoln, NE: Professional Educators Publications.

Snider, W. (1987, June 24). The call for choice. *Education Week, 6*(39), C1–24.

Strother, D. B. (1986). Dropping out. *Phi Delta Kappan, 68*(4), 325–328.

A study of alternatives in American education: Vol. 7, Conclusions and policy implications. (1981). Santa Monica, CA: Rand Corporation.

Toch, T. (1984). The dark side of the excellence movement. *Phi Delta Kappan, 66*(3), 173–176.

Uchitelle, S. (1978). *Policy implications for school districts affording public school options: A case study of results of school choice in one community.* Paper presented at the annual meeting of the American Educational Research Association, Toronto.

U.S. Department of Justice, Office of Juvenile Justice and Delinquency Prevention. (1980). *Program announcement: Prevention of delinquency through alternative education.* Washington, DC: U.S. Government Printing Office.

Walker, R. (1989, April 19). Education "compacts" urged to demand systematic change. *Education Week,* p. 5.

Wehlage, G. G. (1983). *Effective programs for the marginal high school student.* Bloomington, IN: Phi Delta Kappa.

Wehlage, G. G., & Rutter, R. A. (1986). Dropping out: How much do schools contribute to the problem? *Teachers College Record, 87*(3), 374–392.

Wehlage, G. G., Rutter, R. A., Smith, G. A., Lesko, N., & Fernandez, R. R. (1989). *Reducing the risk: Schools as communities.* London: Falmer Press.

Weinstein, G., & Fantini, M. (1970). *Toward humanistic education: A curriculum of affect*. New York: Praeger.

Wheelock, A. (1986). Dropping out: What the research says. *Equity and Choice, 3*(1), 7–11.

William T. Grant Foundation Commission on Work, Family and Citizenship. (1988). The forgotten half: Noncollege youth in America. *Phi Delta Kappan, 69(6), 409–414.*

Yakima Public Schools. (1980). *A demographic profile.*

Young, T. W. (1988). Survey of public alternative schools in Washington. *Options in Education, 3*(4), 11.

Young, T. W. (1989 February). *Alternative schools and teachers: A growing need.* Paper presented at the annual meeting of the Association of Teacher Educators, St. Louis.

Zaltman, G., Florio, D., & Sikorski, L. (1977). *Dynamic education change.* New York: Free Press.

Index

About the Author

Timothy W. Young is Professor of Education at Central Washington University, where he teaches undergraduate methods and graduate foundations courses. He received his doctorate in secondary education from Indiana University in 1980. Previously, he was a social studies and English teacher for six years.

Professor Young has written numerous articles on teaching and learning in *Action in Teacher Education, American Secondary Education, Journal of Classroom Interaction,* and *Phi Delta Kappan.* In addition to public alternative education, his interests include public education in other countries.